Overcome with Paschal Joy

Overcome with Paschal Joy

Chanting through Lent and Easter
Daily Reflections with Familiar Hymns

Mark G. Boyer

WIPF & STOCK · Eugene, Oregon

OVERCOME WITH PASCHAL JOY
Chanting through Lent and Easter—Daily Reflections with Familiar Hymns

Copyright © 2016 Mark G. Boyer. All rights reserved. Except for brief quotations in critical publications or reviews, no part of this book may be reproduced in any manner without prior written permission from the publisher. Write: Permissions, Wipf and Stock Publishers, 199 W. 8th Ave., Suite 3, Eugene, OR 97401.

Wipf & Stock
An Imprint of Wipf and Stock Publishers
199 W. 8th Ave., Suite 3
Eugene, OR 97401

www.wipfandstock.com

PAPERBACK ISBN: 978-1-4982-9273-3
HARDCOVER ISBN: 978-1-4982-9275-7
EBOOK ISBN: 978-1-4982-9274-0

Manufactured in the U.S.A.   JUNE 7, 2016

The Scripture quotations contained herein are from the New Revised Standard Version Bible, copyright © 1989 by the Division of Christian Education of the national Council of the Churches of Christ in the U.S.A., and are used by permission. All rights reserved.

The texts of the hymns contained herein are in the public domain. They may be published and otherwise reproduced without permission. All of them are taken from *Resource Collection of Hymns and Service Music for the Liturgy*, copyright © 1981 by International Committee on English in the Liturgy, Inc., and published by G.I.A. Publications, Inc., 7404 South Mason Ave., Chicago, IL 60638. Also, they can be found in worship aids, hymnals, online, and in many other collections of hymns and carols.

Dedicated to
Pauline Nugent,
nun, teacher, friend

Contents

Introduction | xi

1 Ash Wednesday through Saturday Following Ash Wednesday | 1
    Ash Wednesday | 1
    Thursday after Ash Wednesday | 2
    Friday after Ash Wednesday | 4
    Saturday after Ash Wednesday | 5

2 First Week of Lent | 7
    First Sunday of Lent, Cycle A | 7
    First Sunday of Lent, Cycle B | 8
    First Sunday of Lent, Cycle C | 10
    Monday of the First Week of Lent | 11
    Tuesday of the First Week of Lent | 13
    Wednesday of the First Week of Lent | 14
    Thursday of the First Week of Lent | 16
    Friday of the First Week of Lent | 17
    Saturday of the First Week of Lent | 19

3 Second Week of Lent | 21
    Second Sunday of Lent, Cycle A | 21
    Second Sunday of Lent, Cycle B | 22
    Second Sunday of Lent, Cycle C | 24
    Monday of the Second Week of Lent | 25
    Tuesday of the Second Week of Lent | 27
    Wednesday of the Second Week of Lent | 28
    Thursday of the Second Week of Lent | 30
    Friday of the Second Week of Lent | 31
    Saturday of the Second Week of Lent | 33

4 Third Week of Lent | 35
    Third Sunday of Lent, Cycle A | 35
    Third Sunday of Lent, Cycle B | 37
    Third Sunday of Lent, Cycle C | 38

        Monday of the Third Week of Lent | 40
        Tuesday of the Third Week of Lent | 41
        Wednesday of the Third Week of Lent | 43
        Thursday of the Third Week of Lent | 45
        Friday of the Third Week of Lent | 46
        Saturday of the Third Week of Lent | 48

5   Fourth Week of Lent | 50
        Fourth Sunday of Lent, Cycle A | 50
        Fourth Sunday of Lent, Cycle B | 51
        Fourth Sunday of Lent, Cycle C | 53
        Monday of the Fourth Week of Lent | 55
        Tuesday of the Fourth Week of Lent | 56
        Wednesday of the Fourth Week of Lent | 57
        Thursday of the Fourth Week of Lent | 59
        Friday of the Fourth Week of Lent | 60
        Saturday of the Fourth Week of Lent | 62

6   Fifth Week of Lent | 64
        Fifth Sunday of Lent, Cycle A | 64
        Fifth Sunday of Lent, Cycle B | 66
        Fifth Sunday of Lent, Cycle C | 67
        Monday of the Fifth Week of Lent | 69
        Tuesday of the Fifth Week of Lent | 70
        Wednesday of the Fifth Week of Lent | 72
        Thursday of the Fifth Week of Lent | 73
        Friday of the Fifth Week of Lent | 75
        Saturday of the Fifth Week of Lent | 76

7   Holy Week | 79
        Palm Sunday of the Passion of the Lord, Cycle A | 79
        Palm Sunday of the Passion of the Lord, Cycle B | 81
        Palm Sunday of the Passion of the Lord, Cycle C | 83
        Monday of Holy Week | 84
        Tuesday of Holy Week | 86
        Wednesday of Holy Week | 87

    The Paschal Triduum | 89
        Thursday of the Lord's Supper: Holy Thursday | 89
        Friday of the Passion of the Lord: Good Friday | 91
        The Easter Vigil in the Holy Night: Holy Saturday | 93

8   First Week of Easter | 95
        Easter Sunday of the Resurrection of the Lord, Cycles A, B, and C | 95
        Monday within the Octave of Easter | 97
        Tuesday within the Octave of Easter | 98

Wednesday within the Octave of Easter | 100
Thursday within the Octave of Easter | 101
Friday within the Octave of Easter | 103
Saturday within the Octave of Easter | 104

9   Second Week of Easter | 107
Second Sunday of Easter, Cycle A | 107
Second Sunday of Easter, Cycle B | 109
Second Sunday of Easter, Cycle C | 110
Monday of the Second Week of Easter | 112
Tuesday of the Second Week of Easter | 113
Wednesday of the Second Week of Easter | 115
Thursday of the Second Week of Easter | 117
Friday of the Second Week of Easter | 118
Saturday of the Second Week of Easter | 120

10 Third Week of Easter | 122
Third Sunday of Easter, Cycle A | 122
Third Sunday of Easter, Cycle B | 123
Third Sunday of Easter, Cycle C | 125
Monday of the Third Week of Easter | 127
Tuesday of the Third Week of Easter | 128
Wednesday of the Third Week of Easter | 130
Thursday of the Third Week of Easter | 131
Friday of the Third Week of Easter | 132
Saturday of the Third Week of Easter | 134

11 Fourth Week of Easter | 136
Fourth Sunday of Easter, Cycle A | 136
Fourth Sunday of Easter, Cycle B | 138
Fourth Sunday of Easter, Cycle C | 139
Monday of the Fourth Week of Easter | 141
Tuesday of the Fourth Week of Easter | 143
Wednesday of the Fourth Week of Easter | 144
Thursday of the Fourth Week of Easter | 146
Friday of the Fourth Week of Easter | 147
Saturday of the Fourth Week of Easter | 149

12 Fifth Week of Easter | 151
Fifth Sunday of Easter, Cycle A | 151
Fifth Sunday of Easter, Cycle B | 153
Fifth Sunday of Easter, Cycle C | 154
Monday of the Fifth Week of Easter | 156
Tuesday of the Fifth Week of Easter | 157
Wednesday of the Fifth Week of Easter | 159
Thursday of the Fifth Week of Easter | 160
Friday of the Fifth Week of Easter | 162

Saturday of the Fifth Week of Easter | 164

13 Sixth Week of Easter | 166
   Sixth Sunday of Easter, Cycle A | 166
   Sixth Sunday of Easter, Cycle B | 168
   Sixth Sunday of Easter, Cycle C | 169
   Monday of the Sixth Week of Easter | 171
   Tuesday of the Sixth Week of Easter | 173
   Wednesday of the Sixth Week of Easter | 174
   Thursday of the Sixth Week of Easter | 176
   Friday of the Sixth Week of Easter | 177
   Saturday of the Sixth Week of Easter | 179

14 Seventh Week of Easter | 182
   Solemnity of the Ascension of the Lord, Cycle A | 182
   Solemnity of the Ascension of the Lord, Cycle B | 183
   Solemnity of the Ascension of the Lord, Cycle C | 185
   Monday of the Seventh Week of Easter | 187
   Tuesday of the Seventh Week of Easter | 188
   Wednesday of the Seventh Week of Easter | 190
   Thursday of the Seventh Week of Easter | 192
   Friday of the Seventh Week of Easter | 193
   Saturday of the Seventh Week of Easter | 195

15 Solemnity of Pentecost | 197
   Solemnity of the Vigil of Pentecost | 197
   Solemnity of Pentecost, Cycle A | 199
   Solemnity of Pentecost, Cycle B | 200
   Solemnity of Pentecost, Cycle C | 202

16 Feasts and Solemnities | 204
   February 22: Feast of the Chair of St. Peter the Apostle | 204
   March 19: Solemnity of St. Joseph,
   Spouse of the Blessed Virgin Mary | 206
   March 25: The Solemnity of the Annunciation of the Lord | 208
   April 25: Feast of St. Mark, Evangelist | 210
   May 3: Feast of Sts. Philip and James, Apostles | 212
   May 14: Feast of St. Matthias, Apostle | 214
   May 31: Feast of the Visitation of the Blessed Virgin Mary | 215
   June 11: Memorial of St. Barnabas, Apostle | 217
   Seventh Sunday of Easter, Cycle A | 219
   Seventh Sunday of Easter, Cycle B | 221
   Seventh Sunday of Easter, Cycle C | 222

List of Hymns | 225

Other Books by Mark G. Boyer | 227

Introduction

By the time January comes to an end, most of the Christmas decorations—both those inside the home and outside—have been put away. The announcement is made from the ambo that Lent is beginning or the color on the calendar changes from green to violet, and on the Fridays there is a little fish printed under the purple ink. Lent is a moveable season; this means that its beginning is calculated backward from Easter Sunday.

Since the fourth century, Easter Sunday has been determined by the moon. Easter is the first Sunday after the first full moon after the Spring Equinox. The Spring Equinox, also called the Vernal Equinox, when the number of daylight hours is almost the same as the number of nighttime hours, can occur from March 19 to March 21. Once a person knows when the Vernal Equinox is going to occur, then he or she looks for the next full moon. Once that is pinpointed, then the Sunday following the full moon is Easter, which can occur any date from March 19 through April 25.

Once the date for Easter Sunday is known, then a person counts back six Sundays to find the First Sunday of Lent. The Wednesday before the First Sunday of Lent is Ash Wednesday. Thus, depending upon the date of Easter Sunday, Lent can begin anytime from early February to early March. Once the Lenten Season is figured out, then one works on the Easter Season, which consists of seven full weeks plus one day or fifty days. Pentecost Sunday, the end of the Easter Season, occurs on the eighth Sunday following Easter Sunday.

If all of this sounds a bit too complicated, then all one needs to do is look on a calendar. Most calendars will mark Ash Wednesday, Easter Sunday, and maybe Pentecost Sunday. A Catholic, calendar, however, will also mark all the days in between the beginning of Lent and the end of Easter. The Lent-Easter seasons cover one-fourth of the year or twenty-five

Introduction

percent of the liturgical year. For over forty days, the dark violet of Lent pervades the emptiness brought on by fasting and abstaining. For fifty days, the white of Easter fills the emptiness with joyful Alleluias! The life bursting forth with the nearness of spring with its crocus, daffodils, and tulips cannot match the sweet perfume of Easter lilies. Likewise, the sounds of Lenten hymns in minor keys give way to Easter hymns in major ones.

One of the many things we do as Roman Catholics is sing Lenten and Easter hymns. During Lent, we express our sorrow for sin as we pray, fast, and give alms. During Easter, we shout Alleluias at the end of many hymns to express our praise of God for having raised Christ from the dead. There is no secular form of Lent or Easter, except for maybe Easter dinner. Thus, those who observe Lent and Easter sing religious hymns written for each season. We take time to observe the six weeks of Lent so that our seven-week observance of Easter will be enriched with God's word, prayer, and singing.

We may catch ourselves humming a Lenten hymn that we heard in church on Sunday, especially the old standby: "Lord, Who throughout These Forty Days." We may create a joyful chorus, after observing the solemn Lenten Season, to sing "Jesus Christ Is Risen Today" either alone or with others.

This book, titled *Overcome with Paschal Joy: Chanting through Lent and Easter—Daily Reflections with Familiar Hymns,* presents an exercise for every day of Lent and Easter that combines the daily Scripture texts from the Lectionary for Mass with religious hymns sung during Lent and Easter. The hymns used in this book should be familiar to most Catholics. If a hymn is not known, search online with its title; in most cases it can be listened to with few problems.

"Overcome with Paschal Joy" is a phrase found at the end of all the Easter, Ascension, and Pentecost Prefaces in *The Roman Missal*. Since Lent prepares us to celebrate Easter, it is a fitting title for the ninety days represented by these two seasons.

This book is designed to be used by individuals for private prayer or by families for public prayer. A six-part exercise is offered for every one of the entries.

1. The liturgical day is given, such as Monday of the First Week of Lent. To determine the specific date for a liturgical day, a Catholic calendar should be consulted.

Introduction

2. The daily Scripture texts from the Lectionary for Mass are listed. The reader is urged to review those by reading them from his or her Bible before continuing. If this book is being used for family devotion, various members of the family can take turns reading the assigned passages. For Sundays with A, B, and C Cycles, Cycle A is used in 2017, 2020, 2023, etc.; Cycle B is used in 2018, 2021, 2024, etc.; and Cycle C is used in 2019, 2022, 2025, etc.

3. A verse from a traditional hymn is presented. All the lyrics of the hymns used are in the public domain. If the reader knows the music for the hymn, he or she is advised to sing it or hum it to himself or herself or to sing it as a family.

4. A reflection follows. The reflection is based on the biblical texts and the verse from the hymn in the context of the liturgical seasons of Lent or Easter. The individual may read the reflection, or one person of a family may read it aloud for others.

Throughout the reflections I use the masculine pronoun for God, LORD, LORD God, etc. I am well aware that God is neither male nor female, but in order to avoid the repetition of nouns over and over again, I employ male pronouns, as they are also used throughout most biblical translations.

5. The reflection is followed by a question for personal meditation. The question functions as a guide for personal appropriation of the message of the reflection, and, hopefully, leads the reader into deeper prayer. The fruit of the question may be a simple statement or an idea one lingers with for a few minutes, hours, or days. The process of meditation has no end, but one must take a break in order to attend to the rest of life! After a few minutes of meditation, family members may want to share their thoughts about the question.

6. A prayer concludes the exercise and summarizes the theme explored in the reflection and which served as the foundation for the meditation. One member of a family may say the prayer for all, or all may proclaim the prayer together.

In no Lenten Season or Easter Season will all the entries presented here be used. The last section of this book contains the feasts and solemnities that interrupt or take precedence over the weekdays of Lent and Easter. The best way to know which entry to use is to follow a Catholic calendar.

Introduction

It is my hope that these entries will enable you to hymn your way through Lent and Easter and both come to a deeper relationship with God and a renewed appreciation for these fourteen weeks of the liturgical year.

Mark G. Boyer

1

Ash Wednesday through Saturday Following Ash Wednesday

Ash Wednesday

Scriptures
Joel 2:12–18;
2 Corinthians 5:20–6:2;
Matthew 6:1–6, 16–18

Hymn
Lord, who throughout these forty days
For us did fast and pray,
Teach us to overcome our sins
And close by you to stay.

"LORD, WHO THROUGHOUT THESE FORTY DAYS," VERSE 1

Reflection: The first verse of "Lord, Who throughout These Forty Days" more than aptly summarizes what the Season of Lent is all about. First of all, Ash Wednesday is more than just a day to go to church to get ashes applied to our foreheads! It begins a forty-day period of preparation to celebrate the Paschal Triduum (Holy Thursday, Good Friday, Easter Vigil, and Easter Sunday and the fifty days of the paschal feasts launched by Easter

Sunday). It takes all of forty days to get ready to sustain the fifty-plus-day celebration to come.

We spend these forty days fasting, omitting some amount of food from our daily diet, and abstaining from meat on the appointed days; usually one full meal and two more that do not equal the one full meal is more than enough food for today. According to the prophet Joel, the LORD understands fasting as a means of returning to him with our whole heart. Alongside fasting is praying, not telling God what needs to be done, but listening to what the Holy One tells us we need to do! The best praying is done in one's inner room in secret while fasting according to the Matthean Jesus.

We ask Jesus to remain close to us during these days. His presence can be felt when we give alms—time, talent, treasure—so secretly that our left hand does not know what our right hand is doing! Giving alms of any kind, along with fasting and praying, help us to overcome our sins. Almsgiving gets us out of ourselves; it moves us away from selfishness. And it flows directly from fasting and praying. As St. Paul tells the Corinthians, these forty days are the acceptable time; these forty days are the days of salvation!

Meditation
From what do you need to be saved this Lent?

Prayer
Spare us, your people, O LORD, and create a new heart within us. Grant that our fasting, prayer, and almsgiving may make us more aware of your saving presence. We praise you through Jesus Christ, your Son, who lives and reigns with you and the Holy Spirit, one God, forever and ever. Amen.

Thursday after Ash Wednesday

Scriptures
Deuteronomy 30:15–20;
Luke 9:22–25

Hymn
Take up your cross, the Savior said,

Ash Wednesday through Saturday Following Ash Wednesday

> If you would my disciple be;
> Take up your cross with willing heart,
> And humbly follow after me.

"TAKE UP YOUR CROSS," VERSE 1

Reflection: We don't like hearing the Lukan Jesus make clear that anyone who wishes to follow him must deny himself or herself, take up the cross, and follow him. The word "deny" is anti-cultural enough, and even more so when the word "self" is placed right after it. We live in a culture of indulgence in food, clothes, electronic gadgetry, etc. Have you ever seen a commercial on TV tell you that you may not need the item being advertized? Of course not!

And yet on this second day of Lent the message is deny self. We are to disclaim connection to food, clothes, electronic gadgetry, etc. in order to lose ourselves in service to God through fasting, praying, and almsgiving. Jesus presents the paradox, the seemingly contradictory statement that gushes truth like a fountain. If we save our lives by not denying ourselves, we will lose them; but if we lose our lives through self-denial, then we save them. More importantly, there is no profit in gaining the whole world and losing self in the process. Losing self means losing one's identity, values, character, and uniqueness by being so absorbed into the world that a person no longer knows who he or she is in relationship with God.

Jesus never lost his sense of self, because he lived a life of denying self. He makes that clear when he tells his disciples that he will suffer greatly, be rejected, and killed. Knowing that would be enough for most of us to change course in midstream. That is why following Jesus has to be willed; we have to want to do it. It may bring death and doom, but God has a way of changing those into life and prosperity.

Meditation
Of what do you need to deny yourself this Lent?

Prayer
Ever-living God, you made the tree of defeat into the tree of victory through the death and resurrection of your Son, Jesus Christ. Grant us the strength to

deny ourselves, to take up our crosses, and to follow him in the hope of sharing in his new life. He is Lord forever and ever. Amen.

Friday after Ash Wednesday

Scriptures
Isaiah 58:1–9a;
Matthew 9:14–15

Hymn
As you did hunger and did thirst,
So teach us, gracious Lord,
To die to self and so to live
By your most holy word.

"LORD, WHO THROUGHOUT THESE FORTY DAYS," VERSE 3

Reflection: Fasting is usually associated with not eating some food or abstaining from meat. Some of that kind of fasting is good for us, because it reminds us of our hunger and thirst for God. We do not live on three square meals a day alone; we need God's word to nourish our bodies, too. While self-denial is good for us, the prophet Isaiah presents another kind of fasting that may be better for us.

Isaiah records the Lord GOD stating that some good fasting might involve releasing those we have bound unjustly. These unjustly bound might be people who fall into one of our cultural stereotypes which depend upon the color of one's skin or accent for acceptance. The hungry, the homeless, the naked could also use some setting free from the usual image we impose upon street people. This kind of yoke-breaking fasting will require a lot of self-consciousness on our part and maybe a trip to the local soup kitchen or city shelter to help there. In other words, these types of Isaian fasting means giving away some of our precious time in order to devote it to loftier pursuits.

According to the prophet's God, if we fast from food while carrying out our own business along with the usual quarreling and fighting which that entails, then we've missed the point. We should be carrying out God's

Ash Wednesday through Saturday Following Ash Wednesday

business. Fasting is supposed to leave us changed, altered, or converted. The new version of us that is the result of the fasting proposed by Isaiah lives according to God's word to a greater and greater degree.

Meditation
What kind of fasting do you need to do?

Prayer
Have mercy on us, O God, in your goodness. Fill us with a desire to engage in a fast that will change and humble us. Hear us in the name of your Son, Jesus Christ, the bridegroom of your church who taught us how to die to ourselves; he is Lord forever and ever. Amen.

Saturday after Ash Wednesday

Scriptures
Isaiah 58:9b–14;
Luke 5:27–32

Hymn
Abide with us, that through this life
Of doubts and hopes and pain,
An Easter of unending joy
We may at last attain.

"LORD, WHO THROUGHOUT THESE FORTY DAYS," VERSE 5

Reflection: The word "abide" means "to live or reside in a place." Thus, the fifth verse of "Lord, Who throughout These Forty Days," asks Jesus to live or reside with us during our sojourn on earth. As we journey through this life, which is filled with doubts, hopes, and pains, we look forward to a life of faith, realization, and no more suffering. In other words, we journey toward Easter, both literally and figuratively.

Overcome with Paschal Joy

Literally, Lent is preparation time for the Paschal (Easter) Triduum and the fifty-day celebration of Easter that follows. Literally, we should be hard at work removing oppression wherever we see it, false accusation wherever we hear it, and malicious speech whenever we say it. According to the prophet Isaiah, the result of this literal preparation is light rising out of our darkness. We will be like a watered vegetable garden producing lettuce, spinach, radishes, etc.

Figuratively, we travel toward the Easter that awaits us after we take our last breath. That Easter is one we hope to attain. That Easter will be like the tax collector named Levi, who, after hearing Jesus' invitation to follow him, gets up from his desk, leaves everything behind, and follows him. That dramatic change from one way of life to another results in a banquet attended by a large crowd of infamous tax collectors and Jesus, of course. Jesus makes it clear that he has not come to call the righteous, those who do the right thing because it is the right thing to do, but sinners, with whom he seemed to enjoy abiding!

Meditation
For you, how is Lent a literal preparation for Easter?
How is Lent a figurative preparation for Easter?

Prayer
Through your Holy Spirit, LORD, you abide in your people, filling their darkness with light and bringing forth fruits from their good works. Teach us your ways that even though we may doubt, lose hope, and suffer, we may keep our focus on the unending joy of Easter attained by your Son, Jesus Christ, who lives and reigns with you and the Holy Spirit, one God, forever and ever. Amen.

2

First Week of Lent

On Sundays during Lent there are three entries, one each for cycle A, B, and C, as noted in the introduction. Choose the one that corresponds to the current year's readings.

First Sunday of Lent, Cycle A

Scriptures
Genesis 2:7–9, 3:1–7;
Romans 5:12–19;
Matthew 4:1–11

Hymn
Forty days and forty nights
You were fasting in the wild;
Forty days and forty nights
Tempted, and yet undefiled.

"FORTY DAYS AND FORTY NIGHTS," VERSE 1

Reflection: The Season of Lent lasts (approximately) forty days because, according to Matthew's Gospel, Jesus spent forty days and forty nights fasting in the desert. In biblical literature, forty does not refer to an amount, as is usually understood by modern Bible readers today. Forty is a sacred number, referring to a dignified lifetime. For example, Moses lives to be one-hundred twenty years old, that is, three times forty. Three itself is a sacred number indicating God's presence.

Thus, when the biblical writers state that Jesus spent forty days and forty nights fasting in the desert, they are stating that he spent a sacred time, a lifetime, preparing for his mission. Furthermore, as Matthew narrates the story, Jesus is given three temptations by the devil: to turn stones to bread, to test God's promise of care, and to have absolute power. Jesus, with the strength of divine assistance, resists all three temptations.

He is to be contrasted with the woman and man in the garden in the Book of Genesis; they were tempted by the crafty serpent one time and succumbed to the desire for power. As St. Paul makes clear in his Letter to the Romans, just as they brought sin and death into the world, Jesus Christ brought forgiveness and life. If the disobedience of the first couple imputed weakness to all humankind, then the obedience of Jesus imputed righteousness to all humankind. After his three-fold temptation—contrasted to the single one of the first couple—Jesus remained undefiled, even though he was hungry.

Meditation
What is the greatest temptation that you face?

Prayer
Father, open our lips to praise you for your gracious gift of redemption in the person of Jesus Christ. Justification has overflowed throughout the world. Help us to imitate his righteousness that enables us to resist temptation so that we may worship you in purity of heart. We ask this through the same Jesus Christ, your Son, who lives and reigns with you, and the Holy Spirit, forever and ever. Amen.

First Sunday of Lent, Cycle B

Scriptures
Genesis 9:8–15;
1 Peter 3:19–22;
Mark 1:12–15

First Week of Lent

Hymn

Shall not we your trial share
And from worldly joys abstain,
Fasting with unceasing prayer,
Glad with you to suffer pain?

"FORTY DAYS AND FORTY NIGHTS," VERSE 2

Reflection: In what biblical scholars consider to be the oldest gospel, Mark, only two verses are devoted to Jesus' temptation in the desert. In Mark's account, Jesus is driven there by the Spirit after his baptism, and he remains there for forty days among the wild beasts all the while being tempted by Satan. We do not know what his trial was, as it is presented in its three-fold form in Matthew and Luke, or what worldly joys from which he abstained while in the wilderness. The purpose of the Markan account is to echo the time that the Israelites spent in the desert being formed into God's people. Out of the desert they emerged ready to enter the promised land; out of the desert Jesus emerged with his message that God's kingdom was at hand.

This is why many people associate Lent with the desert. There are no prayer distractions in the desert; a person can engage in never-ending prayer that reminds him or her of his or her baptismal covenant, sealed with water as was the one God entered into with Noah. It is the same God who has washed clean the earth who initiates the solemn agreement with the patriarch never again to repeat his flooding actions. The rainbow will remind God of his covenant.

The annual forty days of Lent serve as our reminder of our baptismal covenant, which either we made or was made for us by parents or guardians. On the day of baptism, a flood washed away all temptation that could draw us away from the saving ark of Jesus. As a sign of the covenant, we were given a candle and told to keep the light burning as a sign that God's kingdom was present with us. Temptation threatens to extinguish the light, but Lent strengthens us to keep temptation from blowing out our flame. Out of the Lenten desert we can emerge on Easter ready to renew our baptismal promises.

Meditation

Besides your baptismal candle, what are the signs of God's covenant with you? What desert experiences of suffering have strengthened your relationship with God?

Prayer

O LORD, you guide us and teach us from the days of our youth, showering kindness and goodness upon us. Through this observance of Lent, grant that our baptismal covenant may be strengthened that we may be found worthy to profess our faith in you and reject worldly desires in the hope of sharing in the kingdom, where you live and reign with your Son, Jesus Christ, and the Holy Spirit, one God, forever and ever. Amen.

First Sunday of Lent, Cycle C

Scripture

Deuteronomy 26:4–10;
Romans 10:8–13;
Luke 4:1–13

Hymn

And if Satan on us press
Flesh or spirit to assail,
Victor in the wilderness,
Grant we may not faint nor fail.

"FORTY DAYS AND FORTY NIGHTS," VERSE 3

Reflection: The word "Satan" first appears in the Hebrew Bible (Old Testament) Book of Job where it means the adversary, the opponent. The satan (notice that it is not capitalized) is a member of God's heavenly court, who sees God's faithful servant Job and proposes to the LORD that Job is loyal because of the many gifts that the Holy One has lavished upon him. Satan proposes that if God were to take away those gifts, that Job would turn and curse the LORD. God accepts Satan's wager, Job is tested, and Job passes, albeit in dust and ashes.

The author of Luke's Gospel does not use the word "Satan" in his temptation account of Jesus being led by the Spirit into the desert for forty days, as does Mark and Matthew. For Luke, Satan is not the adversary; the devil, that is, the accuser or the slander is. That is the role the devil plays in Luke's narrative of the three-fold temptation. Each temptation begins with "if"—if you are the Son of God, if you worship me. But Luke is not finished with this first three-fold accusation. Unique to this author's account is the last verse of today's gospel: "When the devil had finished every test, he departed from him until an opportune time" (Luke 4:13).

So where does the devil reappear? Not only does he specifically enter into Judas (cf. Luke 22:3), but he is also present in the three-fold temptation after Jesus is nailed to the cross. There, the "if" occurs again: if he is the chosen one, if he is the King of Jews, if he is the Messiah (cf. Luke 23:33–43). Just as he was victorious over the devil in the wilderness, so is the Lukan Jesus victorious over the devil on the cross. He does not faint or fail; he hands his life over to the Father, commending his spirit into God's hands. Three days later God raised him from the dead. Like Job before him, Jesus passed the test.

Meditation

What recent test have you passed because of your faithfulness to God?

Prayer

Your strengthening word is near us, LORD God; it echoes in our ears, lives in our heart, and is spoken by our mouths. When we are assailed in flesh or spirit by evil, help us to learn from the victory of your Son's faithfulness. Grant that we may not faint or fail, but praise you in the name of Jesus, who is Lord, forever and ever. Amen.

Monday of the First Week of Lent

Scriptures

Leviticus 19:1–2, 11–18;
Matthew 25:31–46

Overcome with Paschal Joy

Hymn

Praise to the holiest in the height,
And in the depth be praise,
In all his words most wonderful,
Most sure in all his ways.

"PRAISE TO THE HOLIEST IN THE HEIGHT," VERSE 1

Reflection: Quite often, many people think that "being holy" is engaging in specific behaviors, like folded hands, bowed head, kneeling down, etc. While those behaviors may indicate holiness, they do not define holiness. Holiness, according to Moses in the Book of Leviticus, is being like God. Some of those characteristics include not stealing, not lying, not swearing falsely, not robbing, not acting dishonestly, not slandering, not hating, and much more. Since God does not engage in any of those actions, neither should people who want to be holy, who want to be like God.

Uniquely in Matthew's Gospel, Jesus tells a parable that demonstrates that holiness is feeding the hungry, giving drink to the thirsty, welcoming the stranger, clothing the naked, caring for the ill, and visiting prisoners. When a person meets human needs, the person simultaneously meets divine needs! In other words, in serving others, one serves God; one acts like God acts, not distinguishing between people.

When God instructs Moses to tell the Israelites to be holy for he, the LORD, their God, is holy, he has set a goal for people to strive to achieve. We will never be as holy as God is holy because of human limitation. But we can both praise the holiest One in the height, even while knowing that we can never be perfect. His words, no matter if they be commandments or parables, are most wonderful, and his ways are the most sure to achieving some degree of lofty holiness.

Meditation

What does being holy mean to you?

First Week of Lent

Prayer

Your words, heavenly Father, are spirit and life; they give wisdom to your people, enlightening them and filling them with holiness. Let the words of my mouth and the thoughts of my heart find favor in your presence this day. Shape me in the holiness of your Son, Jesus Christ, and that of the Holy Spirit, who live and reign with you as one God, forever and ever. Amen.

Tuesday of the First Week of Lent

Scriptures
Isaiah 55:10–11;
Matthew 6:7–15

Hymn
Praise to the holiest in the height,
And in the depth be praise,
In all his words most wonderful,
Most sure in all his ways.

"PRAISE TO THE HOLIEST IN THE HEIGHT," VERSE 7

Reflection: The astute reader will notice that verse one of "Praise to the Holiest in the Height" (yesterday's entry) is the same as verse seven (today's entry). While yesterday's focus was on holiness, today's is on the wonderful words of God which Isaiah compares to the elements. Just as rain and snow fall out of the sky, watering the earth and making it fertile and fruitful, so does the LORD's words tumble down to us to make us fertile and fruitful. In other words, God's word is effective; it achieves his purpose in sending it.

In Matthew's Gospel, Jesus teaches this same lesson when he instructs his followers not to babble on and on when they pray. God already knows what they need; the purpose of God's word is to inform people of that. For many people, prayer is telling God what he needs to do. However, Jesus instructs that prayer is listening to the Father's words telling us what we need to do. And the list is simple: praise God, do his will, forgive others as he forgives us.

Commonly known as the Lord's Prayer, Matthew's version is much longer than Luke's version, and both differ from the liturgical version which comes from *The Didache*, an ancient early church version that is used during Mass. No matter which version one uses, God is petitioned to give the pray-er what he or she needs for the day: bread, forgiveness, and deliverance from evil. These most wonderful words of God do not tell God anything he doesn't already know; however, they do enable us to praise him in the trust that he will take care of our daily needs, even as they make us fertile and fruitful.

Meditation
What fruitfulness has God brought about in your life through his words?

Prayer
Father in heaven, just as you send the rain and snow to the earth, so do you send your word to our ears, hearts, and minds. Bring your kingdom to fruition within us even as you strengthen our trust in you to provide our daily needs. We praise your holiness in the height for your wonderful words, which direct our steps to you through Jesus Christ, our Lord. Amen.

Wednesday of the First Week of Lent

Scriptures
Jonah 3:1–10;
Luke 11:29–32

Hymn
There's a wideness in God's mercy
Like the wideness of the sea;
There's a kindness in his justice
Which is more than liberty.
There is plentiful redemption
In the blood that has been shed;
There is joy for all the members

First Week of Lent

In the sorrows of the head.

"THERE'S A WIDENESS IN GOD'S MERCY," VERSE 1

Reflection: Mercy is an unmerited kindness or forgiveness shown to an offender or to someone another has power over, such as a judge over a convicted criminal. As demonstrated in "There's a Wideness in God's Mercy," the Holy One does not give people what they deserve; God's mercy is as wide as the sea, as demonstrated in the story of the Hebrew prophet Jonah being sent by God to the pagan and enemy-of-the-Israelites city of Nineveh. Not only does the Mighty One demonstrate that he has a sense of humor in sending his reluctant prophet to preach to his enemies, but God is so moved by the Ninevites's repentance, that he himself repented of what he had threatened to do to them by showing them mercy, which was, indeed, as wide as the sea.

In Luke's Gospel, Jesus presents Jonah as a sign to people gathered around him. Just as Jonah sparked repentance, demonstrated by the people and the animals clothing themselves in sackcloth and ashes and fasting, so Jesus is a sign of the repentance in which we need to be engaged during Lent and during our lives. Because Jesus is greater than Jonah, there is all the more reason for us to repent. In other words, if the pagan people of Nineveh could believe the words of a Hebrew prophet after but one day of preaching, how much more should we believe the words of Jesus after two thousand years of preaching?

The good news of Jesus, indeed greater than Jonah's, is that we have been redeemed by his blood shed on the cross. Through his sorrowful death and glorious resurrection, also signified by Jonah's three days in the belly of the big fish, he has brought the joy of salvation to our lives. We have received plentiful redemption, a liberty which means that we do not have to earn salvation; we need only to accept God's unmerited mercy.

Meditation

What gets in your way of receiving God's unmerited mercy and kindness?

Overcome with Paschal Joy

Prayer

Out of your great kindness, O God, you show mercy to your people, wiping out their offenses with the blood of your Son, Jesus Christ. Grant us the grace to understand the sign of Jonah that we may repent and be cleansed of our sin. We ask this through the same Jesus Christ, who is Lord forever and ever. Amen.

Thursday of the First Week of Lent

Scriptures
Esther C:12, 14–16, 23–25;
Matthew 7:7–12

Hymn
All glory, praise, and honor
To you, Redeemer, King!
To whom the lips of children
Made sweet hosannas ring.
Their praises you accepted;
Accept the prayers we bring,
Great source of love and goodness,
Our Savior and our King.

"ALL GLORY, PRAISE, AND HONOR," REFRAIN AND VERSE 5

Reflection: As can be quickly learned by reading the passage from the Book of Esther, prayer is not telling God what he needs to do. Queen Esther asks God to tell her what she needs to do in order to save the Jews from imminent death. She asks God to put into her mouth persuasive words so that she might convince her husband, the king, to spare her people from the genocide that their enemy has planned for them. Prostrating herself before the LORD, Esther asks, seeks, and knocks on God's door, and she receives his words, finds the courage she needs to appear before the king, and discovers the king's door is open to her request.

While most people sing "All Glory, Praise, and Honor" once a year on Palm Sunday, its last verse summarizes the message of today's biblical texts. Just as God accepted Esther's prayer, we ask the Redeemer, our Savior and our King, to accept the prayers we bring. Those prayers are praises, thanksgivings, for all that God has done in, through, and for us. The great source of love and goodness, God, has lavished us with grace, himself, in the person of Jesus Christ.

The hardest part of prayer is listening; it is very hard for people to stop talking! Listening is difficult because we think that we control our world; each of us thinks of himself or herself as a planet with many satellites that revolve around us. All we need to do is contact the satellite and tell it, him, or her what we want done. This image gets projected onto God. However, when it comes to God, he is the planet, and we are the satellites who revolve around him. We need to learn to listen to his word during Lent so that we know what we should do. Then, like Esther, God's prayer in us will be effective.

Meditation
How much of your prayer is listening? How much of it is talking?

Prayer
Blessed are you, God of Abraham and Sarah, Isaac and Rebekah, of Jacob and Leah and Rachel; help us who are alone and have no one to help us but you. Put your persuasive words in our mouths that we may speak your truth in gladness and do your will willingly. We ask this in the name of Jesus Christ, your Son, who lives and reigns with you and the Holy Spirit, one God, forever and ever. Amen.

Friday of the First Week of Lent

Scriptures
Ezekiel 18:21–28;
Matthew 5:20–26

Hymn
There is welcome for the sinner,
And a promised grace made good.

Overcome with Paschal Joy

> There is mercy with the Savior;
> There is healing in his blood.
> There is grace enough for thousands
> Of new worlds as great as this;
> There is room for fresh creations
> In that upper home of bliss.

"THERE'S A WIDENESS IN GOD'S MERCY," VERSE 2

Reflection: Lent presents us with the opportunity for conversion. Conversion, contrary to its popular understanding of changing from one religion to another or from one church to another church, means to change one's mind which leads to a change in one's behavior. Culturally, we try to change behavior without beginning with a change in mind; a simple investigation of most dieting programs will reveal why they fail: there is no change in the dieter's mind, and, consequently, while behavior may have been altered for a time, once the program is over the dieter reverts to his or her past ways.

The prophet Ezekiel proposes the biblical understanding of conversion. Conversion begins in the wicked person's mind. He turns away from the sins committed, and, instead of dying, he lives. In other words, after changing his mind about what is just and right, he demonstrates the transformation through his behavior. In the words of the second verse of "There's a Wideness in God's Mercy," "There is welcome for the sinner, and a promised grace made good."

In his Sermon on the Mount, the Matthean Jesus presents the same idea. He states that a person's righteousness, doing the right thing because it is the right thing to do, must surpass all others if he or she wants to enter the kingdom of heaven, the upper home of bliss. In this new way of life that Jesus proposes, there is grace enough for thousands of people to be created anew by changing their minds about anger and reconciliation. Instead of saying that it is the other person's problem, Jesus declares that the truly righteous, that is, the truly converted person, knows that he or she must show the Savior's mercy and healing to the opponent. That can only be done by first changing one's mind and then changing one's behavior.

First Week of Lent

Meditation
About what do you need to change your mind and behavior?

Prayer
Out of the depths of depression we call to you, O LORD. Please, hear our voices. Transform our minds with the healing grace and mercy of your Son, Jesus Christ. Then, with your Holy Spirit, inspire our behavior that we walk in righteousness before you. We ask this in the name of him who saved us with his blood, Jesus Christ; he is Lord forever and ever. Amen.

Saturday of the First Week of Lent

Scriptures
Deuteronomy 26:16–19;
Matthew 5:43–48

Hymn
O sacred Head, surrounded
By crown of piercing thorn.
O bleeding Head, so wounded,
Reviled, and put to scorn!
Death's pallid hue comes o'er you,
The glow of life decays,
Yet angels hosts adore you,
And tremble as they gaze.

"O SACRED HEAD, SURROUNDED," VERSE 1

Reflection: In the Hebrew Bible (Old Testament) Book of Deuteronomy, Moses tells the Israelites that they are sacred to the LORD, their God. In Matthew's Gospel, Jesus tells his disciples that their enemies are sacred. And today's hymn is addressed to the sacred head of Jesus. The word "sacred" means dedicated or worthy of religious veneration, worship, and respect. We might substitute the word "special," especially as it is used by the culture in which we live. Thus, the Israelites are special to God. Our enemies are special to us. And Jesus is special for the whole world.

According to Moses' words, the Israelites are so sacred or special to the LORD that he has given them statutes and decrees to follow, and they should follow these with all their heart and soul. This makes them a people peculiarly the LORD's own. According to Jesus, those who do the right thing because it is the right thing to do—that is, live according to the higher righteousness he preaches—love their enemies and pray for their persecutors—that is, consider all opponents sacred or special. They do this because they want to imitate Jesus' God.

As the Matthean Jesus makes clear, God does not discriminate. The Holy One does not only shine his sun on the good and leave the bad in darkness. The Mighty One does not only send rain on the good and leave drought for the bad. No! The sun rises on the good and the bad, and it rains on both the good and the bad. People need to be whole, like God is whole. People need to consider each other sacred, like God considers each person sacred. People need to be aware of how each person is special, just like God knows how each person is special.

Meditation

In what specific ways are you sacred, dedicated, and special to God?

Prayer

Heavenly Father, you make your sun rise and shine on the bad and the good, and you make your rain fall on the just and the unjust. Remove all discrimination from our midst so that we may be whole as you are whole. Grant that our Lenten observance may demonstrate to others the love you have for all people. We ask this through our Lord Jesus Christ, who is adored by your angels forever and ever. Amen.

3

Second Week of Lent

Second Sunday of Lent, Cycle A

Scriptures
Genesis 12:1–4a;
2 Timothy 1:8b–11;
Matthew 17:1–9

Hymn
Take up your cross, heed not the shame,
And let your foolish heart be still;
The Lord for you accepted death
Upon a cross, on Calv'ry's hill.

"TAKE UP YOUR CROSS," VERSE 3

Reflection: In the Bible, God's presence transfigures people. For example, Abram hears God's voice and leaves the land of his kinsfolk, heading off to a land to which the LORD will direct him. Matthew's version of the Transfiguration story describes Jesus' face shining like the sun and Moses and Elijah appearing—quite a feat since both men had been dead for hundreds of years! The second letter of Paul to Timothy narrates the effects of transfiguration: death has been destroyed and life and immortality have been brought to light.

Matthew's account of the Transfiguration serves as a prediction of the resurrection. It is no accident that the scene is set on a high mountain, where God is usually encountered biblically. Moses and Elijah, who obviously have been raised from the dead to be seen by Peter, James, and John, demonstrate that there is life on the other side of death. Even Jesus tells them not to speak a word about this until he has been raised from the dead! As the third verse from "Take Up Your Cross" makes clear, the cross was the instrument of Jesus' final transfiguration from death to life.

Therefore, we should not be put to shame by it. Christians should have a cross in their home. It may be made from two pieces of crossed wood, two large sticks roped together. It may be made from shiny silver or gold. It may have a corpus on it or be plain. Only the foolish Christian fails to look upon the cross daily, but he or she should gaze upon it even more during Lent. The cross reminds us of all our suffering, depression, ageing, and whatever else that accompanies us on our lifetime journey. The cross transfigured Jesus. The cross has the ability to transfigure us.

Meditation
Of what transfiguration experience does the cross remind you?

Prayer
God, you saved us and called us to a holy life, not according to our works, but according to your own design and the grace you bestowed on us in Christ Jesus before time began. With the guidance of your Spirit, gives us strength to take up our crosses that we may be transfigured by them as was your Son, who lives and reigns with you forever and ever. Amen.

Second Sunday of Lent, Cycle B

Scriptures
Genesis 22:1–2, 9a, 10–13, 15–18;
Romans 8:31b–34;
Mark 9:2–10

Second Week of Lent

Hymn

O wisest love! that flesh and blood
Which did in Adam fall,
Should strive afresh against their foe,
Should strive and should prevail.

"PRAISE TO THE HOLIEST IN THE HEIGHT," VERSE 3

Reflection: The wisest love mentioned in the third verse of "Praise to the Holiest in the Height" refers to the fact that God did not spare his own Son, even when Abraham was able to spare Isaac. In other words, the wisest love has all kinds of ways to transfigure people and the world in which they live. Based on Paul's letter to the Romans in which the apostle explains how through one man, Adam, sin and death entered the world, "Praise to the Holiest in the Height" echoes Paul's words about how through one man, Christ Jesus, flesh and blood brought forgiveness and life. Jesus used flesh and blood to prevail over that ancient foe of death. The paradox is that by dying he destroyed death and restored life.

The paradox is found in the story of Abraham being willing to offer his son, Isaac, as a holocaust. Abraham freely entered into the paradox that God can fulfill his promise of descendants as numerous as the stars in the sky or the sands on the seashore even with the death of Isaac. This willingness, this trust of the LORD, brought about a death in Abraham which resulted in the life of Isaac.

Jesus enters into the same paradox in Mark's narrative of the Transfiguration story. Jesus passes into the realm of the dead where he encounters Moses and Elijah, long-dead prophets of Israel. The voice from the overshadowing cloud is like the LORD's messenger to Abraham. It is amazing that not only is Jesus disclosing what the future holds for him—death and transfigured death to resurrection—but that God is present in the flesh and blood of his only-begotten Son. While Abraham's son was spared; God's son, like the ram caught by its horns in the thicket, will become a holocaust. This is so much for Peter, James, and John to take in that they do not understand what rising from the dead could mean!

Overcome with Paschal Joy

Meditation

What wisdom arises for you from the biblical paradox
that death gives birth to life?

Prayer

All-wise God, precious in your eyes is the death of your faithful people. Fill our minds with your truth that death gives birth to life. Help us to learn from Abraham and Isaac, from Peter, James, and John, and from Paul that at the end of our lives we can trust that you will transfigure death into life for us just as you did for your Son, Jesus Christ, who is Lord forever and ever. Amen.

Second Sunday of Lent, Cycle C

Scriptures

Genesis 15:5–12, 17–18;
Philippians 3:17–4:1;
Luke 9:28b–36

Hymn

O gen'rous love! that he who smote
In man for man the foe,
The double agony in man
For man should undergo.

"PRAISE TO THE HOLIEST IN THE HEIGHT," VERSE 5

Reflection: Only in Luke's Gospel do Moses and Elijah converse about the exodus that Jesus was going to accomplish in Jerusalem. Exodus, a biblical word, refers to the great escape of the Hebrews from slavery to freedom under the leadership of Moses. For the author of Luke's Gospel, Jesus' exodus will consist of, first, the great escape from death to life through resurrection, and, second, the great escape from earth to heaven through ascension. The fifth verse of "Praise to the Holiest in the Height" refers to this as a generous love that defeated suffering and death through the double agony of suffering and death.

The Book of Genesis also narrates a type of exodus. God, who has brought Abram to the land he promised to him, seals the deal with a covenant that has the divine presence smeared all over it. Abram is instructed to bring three, three-year-old animals—a heifer, a she-goat, and a ram. The number three is another way of writing about God's presence. Furthermore, the heifer represents God's purity; the she-goat represents God's grace; and the ram represents God's strength. After the animals are split in two, God alone walks through the pieces in this ancient covenant-making ceremony, effectively telling Abram that if God fails to keep the covenant, Abram can cut him in two like the animals. Abram makes his exodus from the ceremony with the promise that his descendants will inherit the promised land.

Indeed, what generous love does God have for people! The transfiguration of Abram and of Jesus is our promise and our hope. As St. Paul writes to the Philippians, we await the day when Christ will transfigure our lowly body so that it conforms to his glorified body. The vision we see today of Abram changed by the LORD's presence and Jesus dazzling Peter, James, and John with his glory is what will occur in us who remain true to a very faithful God.

Meditation
What has our faithful God promised to you?

Prayer
LORD God, your presence fills the universe making you our light and our salvation. Hear our prayer for deeper trust in your promises with the removal of our fears. Keep us as faithful as Abram and Paul and Jesus, who revealed your transfiguring power and lives and reigns with you and the Holy Spirit, one God, forever and ever. Amen.

Monday of the Second Week of Lent

Scriptures
Daniel 9:4b–10;
Luke 6:36–38

Overcome with Paschal Joy

Hymn

For the love of God is broader
Than the measures of the mind,
And the heart of the Eternal
Is most wonderfully kind.
If our love were but more simple,
We should take him at his word,
And our lives would be all sunshine
In the kindness of our Lord.

"THERE'S A WIDENESS IN GOD'S MERCY," VERSE 3

Reflection: The first two lines of verse three of "There's a Wideness in God's Mercy" summarizes the biblical texts presented to us today. God's love is so broad that the human mind cannot begin to measure it. This is why the Matthean Jesus tells his disciples that the measure they use for others will be used to measure them! Thus, they are to be merciful, that is, they are not to give to others what they think they deserve. They are to be merciful as God is merciful. The ways to practice divine mercy are to stop judging, to stop condemning, and to forgive. While none of these are easy, none is impossible.

We can stop judging others by keeping our opinions to ourselves; most of the time we do not know what it is that is motivating another person to do what he or she does. Condemning another can easily be stopped if no judgment is expressed. It doesn't take long, especially in a group of people, for everyone to take sides and expressly condemn one of them. Forgiving may be the most difficult, because forgiveness means responding to some hurt with mercy.

The prayer of Daniel seeks the heart of the eternal God. Daniel begins by reminding God that he is most merciful and kind. The prophet's simple love for his Creator enables him to express his sinfulness and that of his own people in captivity; collectively, they have rebelled and forgotten God's covenant and failed to heed the words of the prophets, who were sent to bring them back to faithfulness. Justice is on God's side; in other words, God has every right to judge, to condemn, and not to forgive. All Daniel can do is to declare that the people are shamefaced, and that they rely totally upon God's unmerited and unlimited mercy and forgiveness. In other words, they must take God at his word.

Meditation
What unlimited love and mercy has God shown you?

Prayer
Merciful God, through your word you have revealed to us that you do not remember our past transgressions, but are ever willing and ready to pardon our sins for your name's sake. Show compassion to us during this Lent and enable us to share your broad mercy with all whom we meet. We come before you shamefacedly through Jesus Christ, your Son, who is Lord forever and ever. Amen.

Tuesday of the Second Week of Lent

Scriptures
Isaiah 1:10, 16–20;
Matthew 23:1–12

Hymn
In this your bitter passion,
Good Shepherd, think of me.
With your most sweet compassion,
Unworthy through I be:
Beneath your Cross abiding
For ever would I rest,
In your dear love confiding,
And with your presence blest.

"O SACRED HEAD, SURROUNDED," VERSE 2

Reflection: There is a very big difference been talking and doing. Lots of people talk, but few people do what they talk about. In one of his most scathing indictments of the scribes and Pharisees in Matthew's Gospel, Jesus tells the crowds to do what the scribes and Pharisees tell them, but not to follow their example of performing works to be seen and recognized by others. In other words, Jesus accuses them of being hypocrites, who preach lofty words but do not practice what they say except to be honored.

The prophet Isaiah tells his readers to put away such practices. The LORD can take their scarlet sins and make them white as snow if they put together the talking and the doing, if they practice what they preach. If they cease doing evil and learn to do good, their crimson red sins will become white as wool. All it takes is a little effort on their part; a statement of unworthiness gets the ball of compassion rolling.

All great religious leaders seek a union between words and deeds because authentic religion is a thing of the heart, that is, of the whole human person in union with himself or herself. Even while the good shepherd, Jesus, endured his passion on the cross, his words matched his deeds. He, the greatest among us, became our servant. He did not exalt himself, but was humbled; out of the depths of God's compassion, the LORD then exalted him.

Meditation

How does talking (preaching) and action (doing) find a union in your life?

Prayer

Good Shepherd, you think of all your people and call them to integrity in your presence. Out of the depths of your compassion, help us to bring together the words we speak and the works we do beneath your cross. May we find confidence in your love and know your saving presence now and into eternity. You are Lord forever and ever. Amen.

Wednesday of the Second Week of Lent

Scriptures
Jeremiah 18:18–20;
Matthew 20:17–28

Second Week of Lent

Hymn

Take up your cross, let not its weight
Fill your weak spirit with alarm;
His strength shall bear your spirit up,
And brace your heart, and nerve your arm.

"TAKE UP YOUR CROSS," VERSE 2

Reflection: The cross should instill fear in us. However, because we see it in churches, in shrines, around people's necks, and on lapels, its fear has been removed. We've cleaned it and made it antiseptic. That makes it very hard for us to hear the prophet Jeremiah's fear when he learns about the plot against him. That also makes it very hard for us to hear the Matthean Jesus' prediction about what is going to happen to him.

The mother of James and John who approaches Jesus and requests seats for her sons on his right and his left is not ready to hear his words about drinking the chalice, a biblical reference to suffering and death. Jesus had just finished teaching that what awaited him in Jerusalem were mocking, scourging, and crucifixion. The mother's request gives Jesus the opportunity to drive home the teaching that any follower of him must take up his or her cross heedless of its weight and without spiritual alarm. The cross is Jesus' way to demonstrate how those who are great are the servants of all others. Jesus' words are lofty, but still do not evoke fear.

The disciples, the mother of James and John, and us are given chalices to drink, that is, crosses to bear. They may consist of illnesses, financial problems, relationship issues, etc. A healthy fear should be present, but looking at the example of Jesus, we find the strength to drink the chalice, to carry the cross. He braces our fearful hearts, confirming our willingness to follow him. He nerves our weak arms, giving us strength not to falter. The easy way is never the best way, as Jeremiah, James, John, and their mother quickly learn; the best way is through the fearful suffering and death to the new life on the other side.

Meditation

What fearful cross have you borne?
How did the example of Jesus strengthen you?

Overcome with Paschal Joy

Prayer

Almighty God, while you heard the cry of Jeremiah, you did not remove his fear of suffering as he brought your word to your people. Neither did you remove the fear of the cross from your own Son, Jesus, as he preached the message of your kingdom. Give us a healthy fear of the cross even as you also strengthen us with the example of Jesus, who lives and reigns with you forever and ever. Amen.

Thursday of the Second Week of Lent

Scriptures
Jeremiah 17:5–10;
Luke 16:19–31

Hymn
When I survey the wondrous cross
On which the Prince of glory died,
My richest gain I count but loss,
And pour contempt on all my pride.

"WHEN I SURVEY THE WONDROUS CROSS," VERSE 1

Reflection: There are two kinds of pride. The first is characterized by a haughty attitude of thinking one is better than others. The second is characterized by a healthy respect for one's self importance, character, life, efforts, and achievements. In the first type of pride, the individual trusts himself or herself. In the second type of pride, the individual trusts God.

Jeremiah compares these two forms of pride to two bushes. The first is like a barren bush in the desert or in a lava waste. The second is like a bush that grows into a tree because it is planted beside a stream which enables it to survive the heat. In Luke's Gospel, Jesus compares the two forms of pride to an unnamed rich man and a poor man named Lazarus. The rich man's pride kept him from seeing the poor man dying outside his door. Furthermore, the expectation that the rich man's wealth guaranteed him blessedness and the poor man's poverty guaranteed him curses is reversed in the next life. In other words, we may have our presuppositions, but they may not conform to God's reality.

The second form of healthy pride enables a person to look at the wondrous cross upon which Jesus died and realize that everything he or she counts among self importance, character, life, efforts, and achievements—his or her richest gain—is really loss, and even a healthy pride is contemptible. In his letter to the Philippians, St. Paul put it this way: "... I regard everything as loss because of the surpassing value of knowing Christ Jesus my Lord. For his sake I have suffered the loss of all things, and I regard them as rubbish, in order that I may gain Christ . . . (Phil 3:8).

Meditation
What happens to your pride when you stand before the cross of Christ Jesus?

Prayer
On the wondrous cross the prince of glory, your Son, Father, died for the salvation of the world. As I gaze upon it, everything that I have gained is now considered loss. Help me to delve into the depths of this truth and to praise you for your wisdom. You are one God—Father, Son, and Holy Spirit—forever and ever. Amen.

Friday of the Second Week of Lent

Scriptures
Genesis 37:3–4, 12–13a, 17b–28a;
Matthew 21:33–43, 45–46

Hymn
Were the whole realm of nature mine,
That were a present all too small:
Love so amazing, so divine,
Demands my soul, my life, my all.

"WHEN I SURVEY THE WONDROUS CROSS," VERSE 5

Overcome with Paschal Joy

Reflection: Joseph, son of Jacob (Israel), was sold into Egyptian slavery by his brothers because they were jealous of him and his dreams. Because of his God-given abilities, Joseph rose to the top of Egyptian society, ultimately reaching the position immediately below Pharaoh. So the result of his brothers' evil deed was God's occasion for a marvelous deed. The whole of Pharaoh's realm was at Joseph's disposal, yet in comparison to the LORD's work it was still too small.

Matthew's version of the vineyard analogy—basically a summary of the history of salvation in story form—ends with the tenants acquiring the whole realm of the vineyard, but even that is too small when compared with Jesus' statement about God's kingdom being taken from the hearers and given to a people who will produce the fruit that the Father seeks. Using Psalm 118:22–23 as another way of saying that God brings good out of evil, the author of Matthew's Gospel states, "The stone that the builders rejected has become the chief cornerstone. This is the LORD's doing; it is marvelous in our eyes." In other words, what is insignificant to human beings becomes great when God gets involved.

The Season of Lent is all about letting God get involved in our lives. For this to happen we have to get uninvolved in our lives. We have to get ourselves out of the way, and prayer, fasting, and almsgiving are proven practices to facilitate that process. Once we get out of our own way, we begin to realize the amazing power of divine love. It demands our soul, our life, our all. When we submit, like Joseph and Jesus, we see God's marvelous deeds taking place throughout our lives.

Meditation
What marvelous deed has God brought about in your life?
What did God require of you to work it?

Prayer
As we recall the marvelous deeds you wrought in the life of Joseph and Jesus, your Son, heavenly Father, we overflow with your amazing, divine love. Send your Holy Spirit to enable us to give you our soul, life, and all that you may work mighty deeds in us. We ask this in the name of Jesus Christ, whom you raised from the dead; he lives and reigns with you forever and ever. Amen.

Saturday of the Second Week of Lent

Scriptures
Micah 7:14–15, 18–20;
Luke 15:1–3, 11–32

Hymn
Troubled souls, why will you scatter
Like a crowd of frightened sheep?
Foolish hearts, why will you wander
From a love so true and deep?
There is welcome for the sinner
And more graces for the good;
There is mercy with the Savior,
There is healing in his blood.

"THERE'S A WIDENESS IN GOD'S MERCY," VERSE 4

Reflection: The parable of the prodigal son is so well known that most people tune it out as soon as the reader begins, "There was a man who had two sons" (Luke 15:11). What we fail to recognize is that it is the third story in a series all dealing with lost and found, namely, a sheep, a coin, and a son. The first two, omitted from today's Lukan Gospel, establish the pattern: something is lost, someone does something ridiculous to find it, and a party ensues. The cost of finding the lost thing is greater than its value. So, one out of ninety-nine sheep is lost; the shepherd stupidly leaves the ninety-nine (who will wander away) to find the one; and then he throws a party that costs more than his lost sheep is worth. The first question posed in verse four of "There's a Wideness in God's Mercy" asks it this way: "Troubled souls, why will you scatter like a crowd of frightened sheep?"

A woman loses one coin; she lights the oil lamps and sweeps the house to find it; then she throws a party to celebrate her find of a coin that would not cover the cost of the oil she burned so she could see to find it. The second question posed in verse four of "There's a Wideness in God's Mercy" asks it this way: Foolish hearts, why will you wander from a love so true and deep?"

And then there is the prodigal father, who declares himself dead by giving his younger son his inheritance! Then, the patriarch sits on his front porch every day looking toward the horizon to see if his son might be walking over the farthest hill. When he spots him one day, he despises his honorable old age by running toward the wayward boy, embracing him, kissing him, clothing him, restoring him to his former position in the family, and throwing a welcome-home party for him. In the words of "There's a Wideness in God's Mercy," "There is welcome for the sinner and more graces for the good." If God is anything like the old father in this parable, then we cannot help but know that there is mercy in the Savior, Jesus Christ, and there is healing for us through his blood.

Meditation
What recent event in your life contained these elements: something was lost, someone did something ridiculous to find it, and a party ensued?

Prayer
Father, like a shepherd you seek the lost sheep of your people, even sending your Son, Jesus Christ, to find them. Have abundant compassion on us and pardon our failings, then we will celebrate your mercy. Hear us through the same Jesus Christ, who lives and reigns with you forever and ever. Amen.

4

Third Week of Lent

In parishes with elect (catechumens) the Cycle A set of Scripture texts may be used in any year.

Third Sunday of Lent, Cycle A

Scriptures
Exodus 17:3–7;
Romans 5:1–2, 5–8;
John 4:5–42

Hymn
Forbid it, Lord, that I should boast
Save in the death of Christ, my God;
All the vain things that charm me most,
I sacrifice them to his blood.

"WHEN I SURVEY THE WONDROUS CROSS," VERSE 2

Reflection: Water is one of those vain things that charm people, mentioned in verse two of "When I survey the Wondrous Cross." Stroll down the aisle of a grocery store to see all the various bottles of charming water. The lack of water in the desert charms the Israelites into grumbling against Moses. However, God has a plan—rather a marvelous deed to enact that will defy explanation; he will bring water from the rock when Moses strikes it with his staff. The flowing water will satisfy the thirst of the Israelites, their children, and their livestock. More importantly, they will know that the LORD is in their midst.

In the unique story in John's Gospel, the Samaritan woman is charmed by water one day around noon when she meets Jesus, who strikes—not literally—the rock and water begins to flow. While resting near the patriarch Jacob's well, a Samaritan woman comes to draw water; the time of the day alerts Jesus to the fact that this is no ordinary woman, since women drew water in the early morning or late evening when it was cooler. Fearlessly, Jesus violates all social Jewish laws about discussing theology with a woman at a well. He keeps tapping her with his truth until water begins to flow from her. We know that water is flowing from her because she leaves her water jar at the well; she is no longer charmed by well water. She goes into town and gushes water over everyone. The townsfolk process to the well, where they find Jesus, who is ready and willing to enable the water of faith to flow from them, too.

The account of the Samaritan woman at the well is in the same gospel that mentions that after Jesus died on the cross, about which we boast, a soldier thrust a spear into his side and blood and water flowed out. And that is why, according to St. Paul in his Letter to the Romans, we boast about the death of Christ. God proves his love for us in that while we were sinners, Christ died for us and unleashed a torrent of spiritual water which fills us with eternal life.

Meditation
What spiritual water has flowed out of you?

Prayer
LORD God, you bring water from rock to satisfy the thirst of your chosen people. Your Son brought water from the life of a Samaritan woman at the well. Give us this living water to drink that we may never thirst again. Grant that it will well up to eternal life. We ask this through our Lord Jesus Christ, who lives and reigns with you and the Holy Spirit, one God, forever and ever. Amen.

Third Week of Lent

Third Sunday of Lent, Cycle B

Scriptures
Exodus 20:1–17;
1 Corinthians 1:22–25;
John 2:13–25

Hymn
And in the garden secretly,
And on the cross on high,
Should teach his brethren, and inspire
To suffer and to die.

"PRAISE TO THE HOLIEST IN THE HEIGHT," VERSE 6

Reflection: ". . . Jews demand signs and Greeks desire wisdom, but we proclaim Christ crucified, a stumbling block to Jews and foolishness to Gentiles," writes St. Paul in his First Letter to the Corinthians (1:22–23). First, Jews did look for marvelous signs of God's presence; even the Johannine Jesus gives many signs, like the one about destroying the temple and he raising it in three days. Second, Greeks, who invented philosophy—which means "love of wisdom"—look for truth that is deeper than many people care to explore. Third, St. Paul proclaims the cross on high, Christ crucified, a stumbling block to Jews, whose Bible declared cursed anyone hung on a tree, and foolishness to Gentiles, whose gods would never choose such a shameful way to die.

What Jesus teaches secretly in the garden and publicly to us is that God is found at the intersection of human foolishness and weakness—a place neither Jews nor Greeks would look! The Johannine Jesus demonstrates this paradoxical truth early in his career when near Passover he drives out of the Jerusalem temple the sheep, oxen, doves, and money changers and then teaches those who would listen about his own suffering, death, and resurrection. His significant words inspire many to believe in his name.

God, it seems, has never been all that interested in animal sacrifices. He only works marvels when absolutely necessary in order to convince his own chosen people that he knows what he is doing. And since he knows all past, present, and future truth, he would not major in philosophy! As the Book of Exodus presents his words, he wants to be loved with no rivalry, and he wants his people to treat each other with basic respect so they can live together in harmony. Commonly known as the Ten Commandments, they seem to present a stumbling block to most people and foolishness to all but a few.

Meditation

Where have you found God? Where has God found you?
Was it in foolishness and weakness or in power and wisdom?

Prayer

Your words, O LORD, are more precious than gold and sweeter than honey from the comb. As we ponder them, help us to know the foolishness of our ways that we may boast only in the cross of your Son, Jesus Christ, who lives and reigns with you and the Holy Spirit, one God, forever and ever. Amen.

Third Sunday of Lent, Cycle C

Scriptures

Exodus 3:1–8a, 13–15;
1 Corinthians 10:1–6, 10–12;
Luke 13:1–9

Hymn

Hear us, almighty Lord, show us your mercy,
Sinners we stand here before you.
Jesus our Savior, Lord of all the nations,
Christ our Redeemer, hear the prayers we offer,
Spare us and save us, comfort us in sorrow.
Jesus our Savior, Lord of all the nations,
Christ our Redeemer, hear the prayers we offer,
Spare us and save us, comfort us in sorrow.

"HEAR US, ALMIGHTY LORD," REFRAIN AND VERSE 1

Third Week of Lent

Reflection: The refrain and the first verse of "Hear Us, Almighty Lord"—in its tenth-century Latin original it was called *Attende, Domine*—summarizes the biblical texts presented to us on this Third Sunday of Lent. The hymn's refrain pleads the LORD for mercy, because all people are sinners. The Exodus narrative about Moses' encounter with God in the form of a burning bush omits the prophet's statement about his unworthiness to accept the mission on which the God of Abraham, Isaac, and Jacob is sending him. All he can do as a sinner standing before the LORD is hide his face in fear before finally agreeing to lead his people out of Egyptian slavery to freedom.

The status of sinner is emphasized by the unique narrative in Luke's Gospel recalling blood-thirsty Pilate's act of mingling the blood of Galileans with Jewish animal sacrifices. Nothing could have been more offensive to Jews, whose law decreed that all blood belonged to God and had to be poured into the earth. Pilate, who was a ruthless sinner when it came to the Jews he governed, dared to violate their sacred commandments. The author of Luke's Gospel adds that event to another one, the collapse of a tower in Siloam on eighteen people, to warn his readers about the need for repentance for sinners.

We—sinners all—stand before Jesus, master of all nations, implore him to hear our prayers and save us, like the gardener who cultivated the ground around a fig tree and fertilized it with the hope that it would bear fruit. We've been given another opportunity for repentance this Lent; if we take advantage of it, we can arrive at Easter bearing fruit. Prayer can cultivate the hard soil of our lives, and sorrow for sins can fertilize our selfish roots. If we do not repent, we may perish like the dead Galileans and Siloamites in Luke's narrative.

Meditation

As a sinner, what mercy do you need to seek from God?
What prayer can you voice to Jesus, seeking forgiveness?

Prayer

Almighty LORD, you hear sinners and show them mercy when they implore your forgiveness. You sent Jesus to be our Savior and to teach us about the fruit that we can bear through a life of repentance. Hear our prayers, spare us, save us, and comfort us through the same Jesus Christ, who lives and reigns with you and the Holy Spirit, forever and ever. Amen.

Monday of the Third Week of Lent

Scriptures
2 Kings 5:1–15ab;
Luke 4:24–30

Hymn
Hear us, almighty Lord, show us your mercy,
Sinners we stand here before you.
Word of the Father, Keystone of God's building,
Source of our gladness, Gateway to the Kingdom,
Free us in mercy from the stains that bind us.

"HEAR US, ALMIGHTY LORD," REFRAIN AND VERSE 2

Reflection: Naaman, the Aramean army commander, has the stain of his leprosy removed by plunging himself into the Jordan River seven times at the word of Elisha, the man of God. However, there is more to the story than at first appears. The Arameans are Israel's enemies, as can be detected by the note about them having captured in a raid a little Israelite girl. Elisha, Elijah's successor and prophet in the land, not only entertains his enemy, but sends him to the dirty Jordan to bathe. As Naaman expresses, the rivers of his home country are cleaner!

The unique scene in Luke's Gospel of Jesus preaching in Nazareth's synagogue further emphasizes this momentous event. As one of his examples of faithfulness to his Jewish audience, he mentions Naaman the Syrian. This riles his hearers, filling them with enough fury to attempt to put him to death. See, what we modern readers fail to understand is that it is not a faithful Jew whom God heals, but the Jew's enemy—and their army commander at that! Naaman, contrasted to Jesus' audience, declares that Israel's God is the God of all the earth—quite a statement by a non-Jewish army commander! Jesus' audience, who has just heard him declare that no prophet is accepted in his native place, enacts his very words when they attempt to hurl him headlong over the hill.

The LORD, Israel's God proclaimed by Jesus, the Word of the Father, the Keystone of God's building, the Gateway to the kingdom, cares for all people—not just Jews, not just Christians, but all people. Even when people discriminate, God does not. Through Elijah and Jesus, he worked marvelous deeds for all people. All they can do is seek him. The refrain of "Hear Us, Almighty Lord"—in its tenth-century Latin original it was called *Attende, Domine*—summarizes the idea this way: "Hear us, almighty Lord, show us your mercy, sinners we stand here before you." That's what Naaman did, and he was healed.

Meditation
Identify a time you acted like Naaman.
Identify a time you acted like those in the synagogue in Nazareth.
What do you notice?

Prayer
You hear the cries of all your people, almighty LORD, and show them mercy. You have satisfied our thirst for you, the living God, in the person of Jesus, your Word, your Keystone, your Gateway. Guide us on our lifetime journey to the kingdom, where we find the source of our gladness and where you live and reign with our Lord Jesus Christ in the unity of the Holy Spirit forever and ever. Amen.

Tuesday of the Third Week of Lent

Scriptures
Daniel 3:25, 34–43;
Matthew 18:21–35

Hymn
Hear us, almighty Lord, show us your mercy,
Sinners we stand here before you.
God of compassion, Lord of might and splendor,

Overcome with Paschal Joy

Graciously listen, hear our cries of anguish,
Touch us and heal us where our sins have wounded.

"HEAR US, ALMIGHTY LORD," REFRAIN AND VERSE 3

Reflection: The phrase, "hear our cries of anguish," from the third verse of "Hear Us, Almighty Lord"—in its tenth-century Latin original called *Attende, Domine*—summarizes the prayer of Azariah in the Book of Daniel. Before proceeding further, the reader needs to be aware that Daniel 3:25, 34-43, indeed 3:24–90 from which the shorter passage is taken, is found only in a Catholic Bible, considered to be additions to Daniel by others. Azariah, otherwise called Abednego, along with two fellow Jews, is thrown into a fiery furnace by King Nebuchadnezzar because they refuse to worship his golden statue. Merely recognizing that there are three young men in the story should be enough to tell the reader that the divine presence, the God of compassion, the Lord of might and splendor, is with them and will save them from the fire.

In his multi-verse prayer, Azariah asks God to demonstrate his mercy by reminding him of his covenant promise to Abraham to make his offspring numerous. Because Azariah and his companions are in Babylonian captivity, they attribute this fact to the people's sins. In other words, they acknowledge that they are sinners. Then, again aware that they are in a strange land with no leader and no temple to offer sacrifice, they ask God to accept their lives as a burnt offering from those who remain faithful. God answers their prayer by not letting the fire touch them. The LORD graciously listens to them and hears their cries of anguish.

Such is not the case of the servant in the unique Matthean story about a king who, moved with compassion, forgives his servant a huge loan. The servant refuses to show compassion and forgive a smaller debt owed by his fellow servant. When tattle-tale servants report to the king what has taken place, he recalls the servant and demands that he repay the full amount. The moral of the story, according to Jesus, is that unless people forgive everything from the heart, the heavenly Father will hold them liable. In other words, after asking God to hear one's cries of anguish and being heard, the one who was heard needs to imitate God and hear and act on the anguished cries of others. Otherwise, the measure one uses will be measured back to him or her.

Third Week of Lent

Meditation
Whom have you recently forgiven? For what did you forgive him or her?

Prayer
God of compassion, Lord of might and splendor, you delivered your servants from the fiery furnace with a great wonder. As we, sinners, stand before you, graciously listen to our prayers for healing. Do not let us be put to shame, but deal with us in your kindness and great mercy. We follow you, we fear you, and we pray to you through Jesus Christ, your Son, who is Lord forever and ever. Amen.

Wednesday of the Third Week of Lent

Scriptures
Deuteronomy 4:1, 5–9;
Matthew 5:17–19

Hymn
Hear us, almighty Lord, show us your mercy,
Sinners we stand here before you.
Humbly confessing that we have offended,
Stripped of illusions, naked in our sorrow,
Pardon, Lord Jesus, those your blood has ransomed.

"HEAR US, ALMIGHTY LORD," REFRAIN AND VERSE 4

Reflection: If we say the words "statues, decrees, and commandments," we usually get a negative response because most people do not like laws, that is, they do not like being told what not to do. Even Moses attempts to soften the impact of the LORD's statues, decrees, and commandments by telling the Israelites that their keeping of the laws will give evidence of their wisdom and intelligence to the nations around them. Moses even hypothesizes that such nations will conclude that Israel is, indeed, a great nation because its God is so close to his people that he even bestows upon them a code of

Overcome with Paschal Joy

law. Well, even Moses' selling job did not convince people to observe the statues, decrees, and commandments.

The Matthean Jesus tried a different tactic, making perfectly clear that he was not in favor of abolishing the law, but he did seek its fulfillment. The law is fulfilled, according to the Matthean Jesus, by practicing a higher form of righteousness. It is not enough to merely adhere to all statues, decrees, and commandments; a person must do the right thing because it is the right thing to do equivocally. In other words, the law must be interiorized. For example, one does not murder others because the law forbids it; one does not murder—Jesus says one does not even get angry at—another because he or she has developed a deep respect for all human life. A person does not need to take an oath to verify his or her veracity; all a person needs to do is be authentic, saying yes when one means yes and no when one means no.

The refrain and fourth verse of "Hear Us, Almighty Lord," attempt to capture this concept of higher righteousness. The standing sinner confesses that he or she has offended Jesus by not living the way he taught. Keeping statues, decrees, and commandments—in a word, law—are not enough; more is required. The sinner has to be stripped of illusions, such as Sunday is his or her day to do whatever he or she wants instead of a day to honor God; after all, it is called the Lord's Day. Then, one appears before Jesus naked in sorrow, seeking forgiveness for not being the Christian person he or she has been called to be. Notice that it is not forgiveness for breaking laws; it is forgiveness for not treating others the way the one who has already ransomed us with his blood desires. If one can attain God's kingdom by keeping statues, decrees, and commandments, then what did Jesus change?

Meditation

How do you live the message of Jesus and, in so doing,
end up keeping God's law?

Prayer

We praise you, O LORD, for your word which spreads over us like snow. With your Holy Spirit help us to interiorize your statues, decrees, and commandments that we may live righteously in your sight. Even though we have been taught by your Son and ransomed by his blood, we confess that we have often lived a life of illusion. But with the strength of your pardon, we pledge to live righteously in your sight. All praise to you, O LORD, forever and ever. Amen.

Thursday of the Third Week of Lent

Scriptures
Jeremiah 7:23–28;
Luke 11:14–23

Hymn
His dying crimson, like a robe
Spreads o'er his body on the Tree;
Then am I dead to all the globe,
And all the globe is dead to me.

"WHEN I SURVEY THE WONDROUS CROSS," VERSE 4

Reflection: The harshness of the fourth verse of "When I Survey the Wondrous Cross" is echoed both in the LORD's words recorded by the prophet Jeremiah and Jesus' words recorded in Luke's Gospel. Quite frankly, God is fed up with trying to get his people to listen to the words of the prophets he sends them. Even though he tries again with Jeremiah, he tells him that they will not listen to him even when he names them a nation that does not listen to the voice of the LORD, its God, or take correction. As far as God is concerned, faithfulness has disappeared from his people; they do not know the meaning of the word; it has been banished from their speech.

In Luke's Gospel, Jesus explains to his crowd of listeners that he drives out demons—the ancient way of speaking about curing people—with the finger of God and brings God's kingdom into their midst. They have been accusing him of casting out demons in the name of Beelzebul, the prince of demons. Jesus explains how impossible and ridiculous that is! How can Satan cast out himself? Even evil knows not to divide its loyalties. Jesus, wielding the power of God's kingdom, is the stronger man attacking and overcoming his enemy. Those who listen to him must make a choice either to be with him or against him.

As the verse from today's hymn makes clear, there is a harshness to the cross that is characterized as red blood flowing out of and over Jesus' body and onto the wood of the cross. Gazing upon this Lenten cross should summon us to open our ears to God's word and his power to heal us of whatever modern demons—alcohol, drugs, internet, phone—possess us. In a way, we will be dead to the world, and the world will be dead to us. However, the practice and mystery of Lent is that we cannot have life until we have died to self and everything and anything that possesses us. That was Jeremiah's message. That was Jesus' message.

Meditation
What harshness do you need to embrace this Lent?

Prayer
Ever-living God, in the person of Jesus you brought your kingdom into the world. As we come before you this day singing your praises and bowing down in worship, we ask you to open our ears that we may hear your voice and be faithful to your ways. We ask this in the name of our Lord Jesus Christ, who suffered the harshness of the cross to teach us the truth that we must die in order to achieve eternal life. He is Lord forever and ever. Amen.

Friday of the Third Week of Lent

Scriptures
Hosea 14:2–10;
Mark 12:28–34

Hymn
See, from his head, his hands, his feet,
Sorrow and love flow mingled down;
Did e'er such love and sorrow meet,
Or thorns compose so rich a crown?

"WHEN I SURVEY THE WONDROUS CROSS," VERSE 3

Third Week of Lent

Reflection: Love is pitched at us from three directions today. First, verse three of "When I Survey the Wondrous Cross" hits us with love flowing down the wood of the cross. The love mentioned in the verse is equated with Jesus' blood oozing from the crown of thorns on his head and the nail wounds in his hands and feet. The hymn's verse identifies the shedding of blood as love.

The prophet Hosea also pitches love at us. Through his prophet, the LORD invites his idol-worshiping Israelites to return to him, and he will forgive them. He declares that he will love them freely, turning away his wrath and drenching them like dew with his love, making them blossom like a lily, enabling them to take root like a cedar tree, and giving them the splendor of an olive tree. The lush garden imagery, sparked by God's love, echoes the first garden created in the Book of Genesis. If the people return to the LORD, his love will be so great that he will return them to paradisiacal freedom.

The Markan Jesus pitches love by quoting the Jewish creed about loving God with the totality of one's being: heart, soul, mind, and strength. However, according to Jesus, that is not enough. One must also love one's neighbor as one's self. The love Jesus pitches to the scribe is self-sacrificing love; it is not the cultural love that is indiscriminately applied to pizza and everything else alike. The love Jesus speaks about is submissive both to God and to others; it is a response to God's overwhelming love of us. That is why the scribe is told that he is not far from the kingdom of God.

Meditation

From which direction do you catch the love that is pitched at you today?

Prayer

Ever-loving God, through your Son, you have revealed that you are love, that you love all people, and that you desire that all people love you in return. Grant us the grace to love you alone with all our heart, soul, mind, and strength, and to love others as we love ourselves. We ask this through our Lord Jesus Christ, who abides in your love and that of the Holy Spirit, one God, forever and ever. Amen.

Overcome with Paschal Joy

Saturday of the Third Week of Lent

Scriptures
Hosea 6:1–6;
Luke 18:9–14

Hymn
Hear us, almighty Lord, show us your mercy,
Sinners we stand here before you.
Innocent captive, you were led to slaughter,
Sentenced by sinners when they brought false witness.
Keep from damnation those your death has rescued.

"HEAR US, ALMIGHTY LORD," REFRAIN AND VERSE 5

Reflection: Some people may think that Lent puts too much emphasis on people as sinners. For those folks today's biblical texts and hymn will be like beating an old drum! However, the fact of the matter is we are sinners when we stand before almighty God, or we are self-righteous and self-justified arrogant people! The Lukan Jesus demonstrates this by telling a parable about two men praying in the temple. To make it even more dramatic, he names one man a Pharisee and the other a tax collector. The Pharisee, a member of one of the more prominent Jewish parties, is a keeper of the Torah, the law, both that which is written and that which is oral or tradition. The tax collector is a Jew who worked for the Roman occupation forces; he made his living by raising the set amount of the Roman tax and pocketing the difference. The Pharisee was admired; the tax collector was detested!

The Pharisee thinks of himself as better than the rest of humanity. He's so good that he even prays to himself! He's not greedy, dishonest, adulterous, or a crook like the tax collector he can see out of the corner of his eye. Furthermore, he fasts and pays temple tithes. Damn he's good! The tax collector knows he is a sinner; bowed down, he beats his breast and begs God for mercy. In the words of the prophet Hosea, he is returning to the LORD. As Jesus finishes his explosive story, he makes sure the crowd understands that it is the tax collector who went home justified, not the Pharisee! Ouch! See, the Pharisee has no need of God; he is self-righteous. The tax collector,

Third Week of Lent

however, knows he needs God's light to shine on him. He is fully aware that he needs God's spring rain of forgiveness to fall upon him. The tax collector understands that God desires love, not sacrifice.

Jesus knew what the tax collector knew. Jesus was the innocent captive who was led like a sheep to the slaughter to demonstrate that God loves to love those who respond to his love. Even when a Pharisee-sinner indicts a tax-collector-sinner, God loves both of them and calls them to return to him and be healed. During Lent, our sinners' prayer is that Jesus keeps all whom he has rescued from self-righteousness, that is, all of us sinners from eternal damnation.

Meditation
Are you more like the Pharisee or more like the tax collector?

Prayer
LORD God, through the prophet Hosea and your Son, you have told us that you desire love, not sacrifice, and knowledge of you, not burnt offerings. Have mercy on us, wipe out or offenses, wash away our guilt, cleans us of our sin. Grant us humility of heart that one day we may be exalted in your presence, where you live with our Lord Jesus Christ and the Holy Spirit, one God, forever and ever. Amen.

5

Fourth Week of Lent

In parishes with elect (catechumens) the Cycle A set of Scripture texts may be used in any year.

Fourth Sunday of Lent, Cycle A

Scriptures
1 Samuel 16:1b, 6–7, 10–13a;
Ephesians 5:8–14;
John 9:1–41

Hymn
Were you there when the sun refused to shine?
Were you there when the sun refused to shine?
O sometimes it causes me to tremble, tremble, tremble;
Were you there when the sun refused to shine?

"WERE YOU THERE WHEN THEY CRUCIFIED MY LORD?" VERSE 4

Reflection: All of the biblical texts on the Fourth Sunday of Lent deal with darkness and light. In John's Gospel, the man born blind lives in darkness until Jesus re-creates him using clay and saliva. Once the unnamed man comes into the light and can see, he begins to realize how much darkness surrounds those around him. His neighbors cannot see that he is the former beggar. The Pharisees cannot see that Jesus would cure on the Sabbath.

Fourth Week of Lent

His parents testify that they have no idea how he can see. Then, the once-in-the-dark man begins to shine light on all those now in darkness by professing his faith in Jesus. Of course, they hate the light and will have nothing to do with it. The question posed by the fourth verse of "Were You There When They Crucified My Lord?" is aptly asked of all those in darkness: "Were you there when the sun refused to shine?" There are so many in darkness that it can cause one to tremble!

While the prophet, priest, and judge named Samuel fills his horn with oil and heads off to Bethlehem to anoint the next king of all Israel, he may as well have filled his horn with light. At first, even Samuel is struck by the appearance in the light of Jesse's seven sons. But God is not interested in muscle men; the LORD wants a future king with heart, that is, one who will be devoted to God with his whole being. When David arrives from the pasture, where he has been tending sheep, God's light shines on him, and Samuel proceeds to anoint him the next king of all Israel.

In the letter to the Ephesians, the author tells his readers that they were once darkness, but now they are light in the Lord Jesus. He distinguishes between activities that are done in the darkness and those that are done in the light. The final act of darkness becoming light will be our light-filled resurrection from the dark grave.

Meditation
Out of what darkness do you need to step this Lent?

Prayer
God of light, through your written word you have spread your light in the world. Through your incarnate word, Jesus Christ, you have taught people how to live as children of light. Fill our hearts with the light of the Holy Spirit that we may profess our faith in the Son of Man, our Lord Jesus Christ, who lives and reigns with you and the Holy Spirit, one God, forever and ever. Amen.

Fourth Sunday of Lent, Cycle B

Scriptures
2 Chronicles 36:14–16, 19–23;
Ephesians 2:4–10;

Overcome with Paschal Joy

John 3:14–21

Hymn

Where you there when they crucified my Lord?
Were you there when they crucified my Lord?
O sometimes it causes me to tremble, tremble, tremble;
Were you there when they crucified my Lord?

"WERE YOU THERE WHEN THEY CRUCIFIED MY LORD?" VERSE 1

Reflection: There is a great biblical truth in the texts presented on this Fourth Sunday of Lent that might cause us to tremble. The scriptural truth is this: God permits evil to happen in order to teach people what he expects of them. This trembling truth is presented first in the Second Book of Chronicles. The chronicler narrates how often the LORD had tried to get his people to turn from their evil ways, but he had no success. So, he permitted the Babylonians to tear down the walls of Jerusalem and burn the temple and the royal residences and take the able-bodied as captives of war to Babylon.

In his unique Johannine dialogue with Nicodemus, Jesus refers to the evil that is going to befall him. He compares himself to the serpent that Moses lifted up in the desert. God loves the world so much, according to Jesus, that he will be lifted up on the cross. His very coming into the world was a gift from God in order to save people. "Were you there when they crucified my Lord?"

The author of the Letter to the Ephesians emphasizes this point. He reminds his readers that once they were dead in their transgressions, but God's grace has saved them. Even though God permits evil to exist, he is always conquering it with good. Once the Persians came to power, Cyrus permitted the Jews to return to Jerusalem and begin rebuilding the city and the temple. After Jesus died on the cross, God raised him to new life. And the same unmerited gift of the new life of grace is offered to those who believe in Christ Jesus.

Fourth Week of Lent

Meditation
What experience of evil in your life was conquered by God's grace?

Prayer
God, you are rich in mercy. Even when evil and transgressions befall us, you pour on us the immeasurable riches of your gift of grace in Christ Jesus. Make us thankful for all your blessings and bring us to the eternal life you have prepared for us. We ask this through our Lord Jesus Christ, your Son, who lives and reigns with you and the Holy Spirit, one God, forever and ever. Amen.

Fourth Sunday of Lent, Cycle C

Scriptures
Joshua 5:9a, 10–12;
2 Corinthians 5:17–21;
Luke 15:1–3, 11–32

Hymn
As you with Satan did contend
And did the vict'ry win,
O give us strength in you to fight,
In you to conquer sin.

"LORD, WHO THROUGHOUT THESE FORTY DAYS," VERSE 2

Reflection: Winning the victory with God's help is the message of this Fourth Sunday of Lent. Verse two of "Lord, Who throughout These Forty Days" reminds us of Jesus' victory over his Satanic temptations in the desert. The passage from the Book of Joshua is about Joshua, Moses' successor, leading the Israelites into the promised land and celebrating a Passover victory meal after they had crossed the Jordan. There is no doubt that Joshua completes the victorious escape from Egyptian slavery begun by Moses. St. Paul, in his second letter to the Corinthians, narrates the victorious reconciliation that Christ accomplished through his death and resurrection.

The message of reconciliation is that whoever believes in Christ is a new creation; all before has passed away. God has reconciled the world to himself in Christ.

Luke's famous parable known as the prodigal son is another tale of victory. First, the old father has a victory when his lost son is found and returns to him. Second, the youngest son has a victory when he decides to stop feeding pigs and return to his father as a hired worker. Even though the son has sunk to the depths of sin, his father hails him as a victor because he is home safe and sound, and, presumably, has learned his life-changing lesson.

The only character in the story which has no victory is the older son. He cannot accept the victory bestowed upon his younger brother by his elderly father. He is so non-reconciled that he will not even enter the house in which he lives because his brother is there celebrating his homecoming victory. He had not read St. Paul's words to the Corinthians about being an ambassador for Christ with the message of reconciliation. His father tries to bring him in, even coming out of the house and pleading with him. But we are left at the end of story standing outside with father and son and wondering if the son will go into the house and celebrate his younger brother's victory meal.

Meditation

Would you or would you not go into the house and celebrate the victory meal? Why or why not?

Prayer

Almighty God, you have reconciled the world to yourself through Christ Jesus and shared with us the ministry of reconciliation. Make us worthy ambassadors of your Son that we may one day share in his victory celebration over death in the kingdom where you live with him and the Holy Spirit, one God, forever and ever. Amen.

Fourth Week of Lent

Monday of the Fourth Week of Lent

Scriptures
Isaiah 65:17–21;
John 4:43–54

Hymn
So shall we have peace divine;
Holier gladness ours shall be;
Round us too shall angels shine,
Such as served you faithfully.

"FORTY DAYS AND FORTY NIGHTS," VERSE 4

Reflection: It is the divine peace and holy gladness mentioned in verse four of "Forty Days and Forty Nights" that help us to understand today's biblical texts. John's Gospel narrates the second of seven special signs that Jesus gives, namely, the healing of a royal official's son because the man trusted Jesus' word. Then, when he had seen the sign, he and his whole household came to believe.

The passage from the end of the Book of the Prophet Isaiah is meant to interpret Jesus' sign. Isaiah writes that God is going to create new heavens and a new earth where there will be no more weeping, crying, or death. This ideal new world has begun in Jesus' sign of healing the royal official's son. It began in the Synoptic Gospels (Mark, Matthew, Luke) when Jesus defeated Satan's temptations and found himself ministered to by faithful angels.

We have seen Jesus' signs and read about them. We have heard Isaiah's words about God's newness. Lent offers us the opportunity to delve ever deeper into what God desires to create in us. Like the royal official, we need only ask and be surprised at the newness emerging from within us.

Meditation
For what do you need to ask to be made new?

Overcome with Paschal Joy

Prayer

O LORD, you change mourning into dancing and death into life. Through our Lenten observance, create new life in us. Bring us to eternal rejoicing and happiness in the kingdom you share with your Son, Jesus Christ, and the Holy Spirit, forever and ever. Amen.

Tuesday of the Fourth Week of Lent

Scriptures
Ezekiel 47:1–9, 12;
John 5:1–16

Hymn
Guard and keep us, Savior dear,
Ever constant by your side;
That with you we may appear
At th' eternal Eastertide.

"FORTY DAYS AND FORTY NIGHTS," VERSE 5

Reflection: The eternal Eastertide mentioned in verse five of "Forty Days and Forty Nights" is prefigured in the water stories in today's Scripture texts. The vision-prone prophet Ezekiel is mentally transported from his captivity in Babylon to the entrance of the destroyed temple in Jerusalem. There he sees water flowing toward the east, the place of sunrise, light, Easter! Every time he measures the water, he discovers that it is getting deeper and deeper; it floods away all that is evil and gives life to everything growing alongside its course, even making the salt water fresh and causing the trees to produce fruit every month! Truly, this is amazing water, eternal Eastertide water!

In John's Gospel, Jesus works a sign near the pool named Bethesda. A man who has suffered illness for thirty-eight years had waited for someone to plunge him into the healing waters, but he could never get into the pool because it filled so quickly with others who were ill, blind, lame, and crippled. All Jesus does is tell him to rise, pick up the mat he is lying on, and walk. The healed man doesn't even know that it is Jesus of Nazareth who has bathed him in the eternal Easter waters without even getting him wet!

One of the themes running through the Lenten Scripture texts is baptism. Baptism plunges a person into the paschal mystery, the death and resurrection of Jesus. It not only washes the person clean, but it fills him or her to overflowing with new life, as seen in Ezekiel's vision. As a result the person produces abundant fruit. Baptism also heals the person of all past sin. It guards and keeps us; the risen Christ, into whose death and resurrection we have been immersed, is ever at our side, filling us with eternal life now even as await its fullness when we appear with him in the eternal Easter.

Meditation
What aspect of water—destruction, life, healing, etc.—
gets most of your attention?
How does that aspect of water inform your spirituality?

Prayer
Savior, Son of God, you guard and keep your people who have plunged into the mystery of your own death and resurrection. Deepen our appreciation of the watery, Easter sacrament of baptism and grant that one day we may share fully in your resurrected life. You live and reign with the Father and the Holy Spirit, one God, forever and ever. Amen.

Wednesday of the Fourth Week of Lent

Scriptures
Isaiah 49:8–15;
John 5:17–30

Hymn
Were you there when they pierced him in the side?
Were you there when they pierced him in the side?
O sometimes it causes me to tremble, tremble, tremble;
Were you there when they pierced him in the side?

Overcome with Paschal Joy

"WERE YOU THERE WHEN THEY CRUCIFIED MY LORD?" VERSE 3

Reflection: Unique to John's Gospel is the scene of Jesus' side being pierced by a soldier with a lance after he dies on the cross. The piercing of Jesus' side serves two purposes: physically, to ensure that he is dead, and, theologically, to announce that out of his side, like out of Adam's side came woman, comes the church in terms of water (baptism) and blood (eucharist). The narrator of John's Gospel explains why Jesus' opponents, the Jews, tried to kill him; he broke the sabbath by working on it, and he called God his Father, making himself equal to God. This latter claim, from a Jewish point of view, is called blasphemy.

In the passage assigned for today from John's Gospel, Jesus declares that physical death is not the end of existence. The Father raises the dead and gives life, states Jesus. The dead hear the voice of the Son of God, and those who hear live. Furthermore, all who are in the tombs, the dead, hear the voice of the Son of Man and will come out. Those who had done good deeds will experience resurrection; those who have done wicked deeds will be condemned. All of this will be the result of Jesus' side being pierced. From out of his side there flowed abundant life (water) and nourishment (blood).

This concept of human restoration is also found in the prophet Isaiah. Through Isaiah's words, the LORD reminds his people that just like a mother cannot forget the child to whom she has given birth, so he cannot forget the people he called to be his own. He is bound to them in covenant. He will restore them and their land. The hope for restoration of land and the hope for life on the other side of death is sustained in us through water and blood from the pierced side of Jesus on the cross. Every time we enter a church, we dip our hand into the baptismal font and, especially during Lent, remember the restoration given us by that water. We approach the chalice containing the blood of Christ and drink the very stuff of life that is pumped by our heart throughout our bodies. These simple, but profound, actions should cause us to tremble, tremble, tremble.

Meditation

In what specific ways can you deepen your appreciation
for the hope you receive from the water and blood

flowing from the side of Christ on the cross.

Prayer

While we were not there when the soldier pierced the side of your Son, LORD God, we do share in the hope of eternal life that continues to flow from your church. Strengthen our covenant with you that we may do good works all our days and come to the resurrected life you share with Jesus Christ and the Holy Spirit forever and ever. Amen.

Thursday of the Fourth Week of Lent

Scriptures
Exodus 32:7–14;
John 5:31–47

Hymn
And through these days of penitence,
And through your passiontide,
For ever more, in life and death,
O Lord with us abide.

"LORD, WHO THROUGHOUT THESE FORTY DAYS," VERSE 4

Reflection: The word "passiontide" in verse four of "Lord, Who throughout These Forty Days" has nothing to do with emotions. It refers to the last two weeks of Lent, namely, the Fifth Sunday of Lent to Easter. "Passiontide" represents the lifelong struggle between life and death. From the moment we are born until the day we draw our last breath, we are engaged in the struggle. Illness, age, and suffering of any kind threaten our lives, and so we use every means available to maintain life and keep death at bay for as long as we can.

There is also the spiritual struggle between life and death. The Season of Lent is focused on penitence, which refers to regret or sorrow for sins and misdeeds. This is the struggle between eternal life and eternal death.

The biblical passage from the Book of Exodus illustrates the Israelites' repentance for having made and worshiped a molten calf. Moses pleads with God to relent in punishing his people for their sin. The LORD hears Moses' cry and relents in the punishment he had threatened to inflict on the people. And he does the same for us.

We ask God to abide with us, to stay with us, even though we are sinners, often headed towards eternal death. We ask the community of believers to pray for us during Lent, after confessing to that assembly that we have greatly sinned in what we have done and what we have failed to do. Through prayer, fasting, and almsgiving, we engage in penitence so that we can be strengthened to enter with Jesus into the last two weeks of his struggle between life and death. Just as the LORD did not abandon the people he had led from slavery to freedom, and just as Jesus did not abandon the people he had come to save, so God does not abandon those who maintain the struggle between life and death, both physically and spiritually.

Meditation

What is your greatest physical struggle between life and death?
What is your greatest spiritual struggle between life and death?

Prayer

O Lord, abide with us throughout these days of penitence when life and death struggle against each other. Through our works of penitence, strengthen us both in body and spirit that we may follow faithfully your Son, Jesus Christ, whom you sent and in whom we believe. He is Lord forever and ever. Amen.

Friday of the Fourth Week of Lent

Scriptures
Wisdom 2:1a, 12–22;
John 7:1–2, 10, 25–30

Hymn
O loving wisdom of our God!
When all was sin and shame,

Fourth Week of Lent

A second Adam to the fight
And to the rescue came.

"PRAISE TO THE HOLIEST IN THE HEIGHT," VERSE 2

Reflection: Many people understand wisdom to refer to intelligence. Those who study and earn all kinds of degrees—both undergraduate and graduate—are considered to be wise people. Biblical wisdom, however, has nothing to do with one's Intelligent Quotient; biblical wisdom names truth. It puts into words those deep universal truths about life that many people never investigate. Verse two of "Praise to the Holiest in the Height" identifies one of these truths. When the world was falling apart at the seams, God, in his wisdom, decided to start over with a new Adam, Jesus Christ, who did what the first Adam had not done, namely, obey God. The new Adam obeyed his Father all the way to his death on the cross, demonstrating to humankind that God rescues those who learn the wisdom that it is through death that life arises. Because of Jesus' faithfulness, God raised him for the dead.

The passage from the Book of Wisdom presents the foolishness of the wicked as compared to the wisdom of the just. Even though the wicked establish ways to destroy the just, the wicked do not plumb the depths of God's wisdom. Their wickedness blinds them; their focus is too narrow. As the biblical text makes clear, the wicked do not know the hidden counsels of God, that is, they do not know God's wisdom. They have not counted on the recompense that God offers to the innocent and wisely faithful.

The same point is made in the greatly edited text from John's Gospel. The wicked, here identified with the Jews, are trying to kill Jesus because he upsets their picture of how God works. Jesus maintains his innocent wisdom by speaking openly and continuing to teach. His enemies, who continue to seek ways to arrest him, fail to recognize that his hour has not yet come. He knows who sent him, and his wisdom enables him to do his works and to preach his message. He also knows the truth that God gives life to those who risk death in his service.

Meditation
What wisdom does today's biblical texts reveal to you?

Overcome with Paschal Joy

Prayer

All-knowing God, when your world had fallen into sin and shame, you sent your word, your wisdom, Jesus Christ, as a second Adam to rescue the human family. Through his ministry and preaching, he disclosed the deeper truths of your wisdom that we might be set free. Hear our prayer for enlightenment this day, and guide us through Lent to Easter. We ask this through the same Christ our Lord. Amen.

Saturday of the Fourth Week of Lent

Scriptures
Jeremiah 11:18–20;
John 7:40–53

Hymn
Crown him with many crowns,
The Lamb upon his throne;
Hark! How the heav'nly anthem drowns
All music but its own:
Awake, my soul, and sing,
He died to set us free;
Now hail him as your glorious king
Through all eternity.

"CROWN HIM WITH MANY CROWNS," VERSE 1

Reflection: The first verse of "Crown Him with Many Crowns" not only bestows much to contemplate, but it also summarizes the biblical texts presented to us on this last day of the Fourth Week of Lent. The prophet Jeremiah refers to himself as a trusting lamb led to slaughter, emphasizing the fact that like the lamb does not know that it will be the main course for dinner, the prophet did not know that those to whom he had been sent were hatching plots against his life. Jesus, the Lamb upon his throne in the hymn, is the slaughtered man whom God raised from the dead.

Fourth Week of Lent

While we do not know the words of the heavenly anthem that drowns all other music, we do have the biblical psalm or song that expresses our refuge in the LORD. The singer seeks to be saved from his pursuers because he is innocent, as God can see by searching his heart and soul. We, who like Jeremiah know that the LORD is a just judge, a searcher of mind and heart, trust that the Holy One will save the upright among whom we hope to be numbered.

The One who died to set us free is the subject of controversy in John's Gospel. Some people are declaring him to be the prophet, that is, the prophet for whom Moses hoped would one day come into the world to succeed him. Others are declaring him to be the anointed, the one God had chosen, like the kings of Judah of old. This last claim presents a problem; God's anointed was not supposed to come from Galilee, as Jesus did, but from Bethlehem, as David did. We crown him with many crowns and hail him as our glorious king; he reigns throughout eternity.

Meditation
What is your favorite way to describe Jesus: as a slaughtered lamb, as the lamb upon a throne, as a great prophet, or as the anointed? What does your choice mean to you?

Prayer
Like a trusting lamb led to the slaughter was your Son, heavenly Father, as he mounted the cross to set free all people. As we awaken our souls to sing your praises, hear our earthly anthems that crown the crucified One with many crowns; he is our glorious king both now and forever and ever. Amen.

6

Fifth Week of Lent

In parishes with elect (catechumens) the Cycle A set of Scripture texts may be used in any year.

Fifth Sunday of Lent, Cycle A

Scriptures
Ezekiel 37:12–14;
Romans 8:8–11;
John 11:1–45

Hymn
Take up your cross, then, in his strength,
And calmly ev'ry danger brave;
It guides you to a better home
And leads to vict'ry o'er the grave.

"TAKE UP YOUR CROSS," VERSE 4

Reflection: The phrase, "victory over the grave," in verse four of "Take Up Your Cross" aptly summarizes the biblical texts presented to us on this Fifth Sunday of Lent, the beginning of Passiontide. In one of his visions of dry human bones spread over a plain, the prophet Ezekiel watches as God joins the bones together, puts flesh on them, and blows the wind of spirit into them. Then, the Lord GOD declares that he is going to open the graves of the Israelites and bring them to life. Grave is a euphemism for captivity; in other words, God is going to bring his people out of Babylonian and Persian captivity and restore them to their land.

Ezekiel's vision is chosen to echo the unique Johannine story of Jesus raising Lazarus from the grave. However, Lazarus gets too much attention by the reader, who often fails to recognize that it is the dead man's sister Mary who, by professing her deep faith in Jesus, sparks the faith of many Jews who come to believe in him. By carefully observing the text, the reader will notice that Martha initially does profess faith, but then doubts greatly when Jesus orders the stone covering the tomb's entrance to be removed.

It is St. Paul in his Letter to the Romans who best presents today's message with his contrast between flesh and spirit. Faith and baptism into Christ destroy the desires of the flesh and fill one with the promptings of the spirit. Paul's conclusion is that the indwelling of Christ in those of spirit serves as a promise of victory over the grave. If the Spirit of God who raised Christ from the dead dwells in us, then the same God who raised Christ from the dead will also raise us from the grave through the Spirit dwelling in us. Thus, we have no fear of taking up our cross and braving every danger, because we have the pledge of a better home, one that begins with victory over the grave.

Meditation

Using grave as an image, what grave has God opened for you?
In other words, in what death-defying event did you engage and emerge alive?

Prayer

LORD of all life, you promised your people that you would open their graves and have them rise from them, and for Jesus, your Son, you rolled back the stone to the entrance of his tomb and raised him to new life. Grant that we, after being conformed to him through water and Spirit in baptism, may have immortal life given to our bodies after mortal death. We ask this through the same Jesus Christ, who lives and reigns with you and the Holy Spirit, one God, forever and ever. Amen.

Overcome with Paschal Joy

Fifth Sunday of Lent, Cycle B

Scriptures
Jeremiah 31:31–34;
Hebrews 5:7–9;
John 12:20-33

Hymn
Were you there when they laid him in the tomb?
Were you there when they laid him in the tomb?
O sometimes it causes me to tremble, tremble, tremble;
Were you there when they laid him in the tomb?

"WERE YOU THERE WHEN THEY CRUCIFIED MY LORD?" VERSE 5

Reflection: Using metaphorical language, the Johannine Jesus declares that his hour has come, that is, it will not be long before he is crucified and laid in a tomb. Jesus compares his imminent death to a grain of wheat that remains such unless it falls to the ground, is buried by soil, dies, and then rises to produce a whole head of grains of wheat. In other words, death gives birth to abundant life. When he is lifted up on the cross and dies, his resurrection to new life will draw many to him.

The passage from the Letter to the Hebrews portrays Jesus' humanity. Before he dies he offers prayers and supplications to his Father, who is able to save him from death, but does not desire to do so. For the author of Hebrews, the major purpose of Jesus' death is to learn obedience to God through the discipline of suffering. The image is that of an athlete, who suffers greatly in order to become perfect at his or her sport. Because of Jesus' reverence, God raises Jesus from the dead and makes him the source of eternal salvation for all who obey him.

The death and resurrection of Jesus is the new covenant mentioned by the prophet Jeremiah. It is not written on tablets of stones; rather, it is carved upon people's hearts. Here, Jeremiah is indicating that the solemn agreement that God has entered into with people is written on the totality of their being. The LORD desires that they give their total selves to him, just like Jesus gave his total self to God. It is through the free donation of self to the Creator that one dies and watches as his or her grain of wheat sprouts and produces much fruit. Once a person becomes aware of this process, how can he or she help but tremble?

Meditation
What of you is like a grain of wheat that has fallen into the earth, died, grown, and produced much fruit?

Prayer
Like a grain of wheat, your Son, LORD God, died on the cross and was buried deep into the earth. After three days you raised him to new life and drew many people to him in a new covenant of your love. Give us a great appreciation for this mystery. When the hour of death approaches, give us the confidence to trust that you will bring forth an abundant harvest from the grain of wheat of our lives. We ask this in the name of Jesus Christ, who is Lord forever and ever. Amen.

Fifth Sunday of Lent, Cycle C

Scriptures
Isaiah 43:16–21;
Philippians 3:8–14;
John 8:1–11

Hymn
Humbled for a season
To receive a name
From the lips of sinners
Unto whom he came,
Faithfully he bore it
Spotless to the last,
Brought it back victorious
When from death he passed.

"AT THE NAME OF JESUS," VERSE 4

Overcome with Paschal Joy

Reflection: Verse four of "At the Name of Jesus" sets the "moving forward" theme of the biblical texts presented on this Fifth Sunday of Lent. After being humbled on the cross, Jesus was named Lord by sinners. He kept moving forward, faithfully bearing his saving name all the way to the cross, into the grave, and out of the grave. The passage from the prophet Isaiah records the LORD saying that he is moving forward with a new exodus. Like the first exodus from Egyptian slavery, the new exodus from Babylonian captivity will feature water in the desert and rivers in the wasteland from which his people can drink.

In his Letter to the Philippians, St. Paul is moving forward in pursuit of his goal, the prize of God's upward calling in Christ Jesus. Like Isaiah before him who said not to remember the things of the past, Paul looks at the past as rubbish. The righteousness based on the observance of Torah that he once thought he had is past. He tells the Philippians that he is moving forward with his faith in Christ and the righteousness that comes from God. His hope is that he will one day also receive resurrection from the dead.

The Johannine Jesus is also moving forward in today's passage. A woman has been caught in adultery, a crime punishable in Judaism by stoning to death. However, Jesus is ready to move forward, and does so by questioning the unnamed woman's accusers. They dare not answer, and so one by one they leave. Then, Jesus tells the woman to move forward and to sin no more as an example of the moving forward that we need to be doing during Lent. Instead of getting caught up in the past—this is the way we used to do it or this is the way it has always been done—Lent presents us with the opportunity to move forward and enjoy the new life attested to by Isaiah, Paul, and Jesus.

Meditation

From what past do you need to move forward in order to experience new life?

Prayer

O LORD, you have done great things for your people throughout history, but these cannot compare to the greater things you have done in Jesus, your Son, and the greatest things you continue to do today. Hear this prayer from the lips of sinners: Send your Holy Spirit to help us move forward that we may one day come rejoicing into the kingdom, where you live with Jesus Christ and the Holy Spirit, one God, forever and ever. Amen.

Monday of the Fifth Week of Lent

Scriptures
Daniel 13:1–9, 15–17, 19–30, 33–62;
John 8:1–11 (Years A and B);
John 8:12–20 (Year C)

Hymn
Crown him the Son of God
Before all worlds began:
And you who tread where he has trod
Crown him the Son of man;
Who ev'ry grief has known
That wrings the human breast,
And takes and bears them for his own
That all in him may rest.

"CROWN HIM WITH MANY CROWNS," VERSE 2

Reflection: The grief that wrings the human breast is obvious in the extremely long story about Susanna, daughter of Hilkiah and wife of Joakim. The account is set during the Babylonian captivity of the Jews. Basically, upright Susanna is met by two judges of Israel who want to lie with her, but she refuses their advance. Because she refuses to sleep with them, the two Jewish elders accuse Susanna of meeting a young man in the garden and, thus, cheating on her husband by sleeping with him. Because of the presumed uprightness of the judges, their testimony is accepted as fact, and Susanna is condemned to death—until God stirs up the spirit of young Daniel.

Daniel has been crowned by God with wisdom. In order to get to the truth of the matter, he separates the two elders and questions each separately to determine under what tree they found Susanna with the young man.

Each gives a different answer, thus indicting himself and declaring Susanna to be not guilty. Because the elders were found to be guilty of perjury, they received the sentence they had decreed for Susanna.

Daniel's wise interrogation of the elders is meant to prepare for the wisdom of Jesus in John's Gospel. When confronting scribes and Pharisees with a woman caught in adultery, he tells them that the person who has never sinned can pick up and throw the first stone. Then he challenges the same scribes and Pharisees to display their wisdom by following him and walking in the light. They accuse him of having the power of testimony of only one, when two people are needed. He reminds them that he and the Father are two, who bear testimony to the truth. As Jesus—and Daniel before him—makes clear, it may take a while to arrive at the real truth. We crown his wisdom by calling him Son of God, the one who has existed before the world began, and Son of man, the one who walked the earth upon which we live.

Meditation
Recently, when have you had to delve deeper into a matter to discover the real truth?

Prayer
Eternal God, you know what is hidden, and you are aware of all things before they come to be. Guide us to the depth of your truth by sending us the Holy Spirit as you once sent him to the prophet Daniel. We ask this through our Lord Jesus Christ, your Son, who lives and reigns with you and the Holy Spirit, one God, forever and ever. Amen.

Tuesday of the Fifth Week of Lent

Scriptures
Numbers 21:4–9;
John 8:21–30

Hymn
Take up your cross, and follow Christ,

Fifth Week of Lent

> Nor think till death to lay it down;
> For only those who bear the cross
> May hope to wear the glorious crown.
>
> "TAKE UP YOUR CROSS," VERSE 5

Reflection: The cross permeates this Tuesday of the Fifth Week of Lent. We find it in the hymn, which tells us to take up our cross and follow Jesus. We should not give even a thought to laying it down. We bear it throughout our lives; it may consist of a physical abnormality, a mental issue, or a spiritual problem. Nothing should dampen our hope of wearing the glorious crown that awaits us at the end of our journey. God has demonstrated his faithfulness in the person of Jesus, who carried his cross to death; then, God raised him from the dead.

The cross is found in a disguised form in the Book of Numbers. Because the Israelites were complaining about the length of their journey and their lack of food and water in the desert, God punished them by sending poisonous snakes among them. In other words, they walked right into a snake pit! God instructs Moses to make a bronze snake and mount it on a pole; anyone bitten can look at it and be healed. While the bronze serpent was ultimately destroyed by one of the future kings of Israel, we still see this sign today. It is known as a caduceus. The snake or snakes wound around a pole can be found on ambulances, in hospitals, and in doctors' offices.

Jesus himself uses this image specifically in dialogue with Nicodemus. Indirectly, he also refers to it in today's passage from John's Gospel. He speaks about being lifted up, which means both lifted up on the cross and lifted up to the Father from whom he came. He tells his listeners that once he is lifted up, they will realize that he is God (I AM) and that he does what the Father has told him to do. Thus, the Son of Man takes up the cross so that the Son of God may be lifted up.

Meditation

What cross has God given you to bear?
How often have you been lifted up on it?

Overcome with Paschal Joy

Prayer

God of the cross, you healed your people who were bitten by serpents in the desert through the bronze serpent on a pole. You healed all people through your Son lifted up on the cross. Give us the strength to bear whatever cross you have entrusted to us that one day we may come to share in the glory of the resurrection. Jesus is Lord forever and ever. Amen.

Wednesday of the Fifth Week of Lent

Scriptures
Daniel 3:14–20, 91–92, 95;
John 8:31–42

Hymn
Holy God, we praise thy Name;
Lord of all, we bow before thee!
All on earth thy scepter claim,
All in heav'n above adore thee;
Infinite thy vast domain,
Everlasting is thy reign.

"HOLY GOD, WE PRAISE THY NAME," VERSE 1

Reflection: In this middle day of the Fifth Week of Lent, we stop for a moment and break into praise of God. "Blessed are you, O Lord, God of our ancestors, and to be praised and highly exalted forever" (Dan 3:52a), begins the Responsorial Psalm, consisting of six of the verses that were edited from today's account of the three Jewish young men tossed into Nebuchadnezzar's fiery furnace because they would not fall down in worship of the golden statue that he had made. Even the account of their being tossed into the fire oozes with praise. There are three of them, the number that represents God. And when the king peers into the furnace and sees four men, the number that represents the earth, well, there is nothing left to do but to praise the LORD, the God of heaven and earth. Even Nebuchadnezzar ends up praising the God of the three young men he had tried to kill!

Fifth Week of Lent

Today's hymn, if it had been written when Nebuchadnezzar walked on the earth, would have been sung: Holy God, we praise your name. Lord of all, we bow before you. All on earth your scepter claim, all in heaven above adore you. Infinite is your vast domain; everlasting is your reign. The three young men in the furnace bless God's holy and glorious name. They bless God in his temple, on his throne, and in heaven. He is praiseworthy and exalted and glorious forever.

In John's Gospel, Jesus sings the praises of those Jews who have come to believe in him. He reminds them that if they remain in his word, they will know the truth, and the truth will set them free from their sins; but they are still trying to kill him because they declare that they are descendants of Abraham and have no need to be set free. Even though they have come to believe in Jesus, his word has no room among them. If it did, they would be doing the works of Abraham. Then, they would be as free as the three young men in the furnace to sing God's praises.

Meditation
For what do you need to praise God today?

Prayer
Ever-holy God, we praise your name and bow before you in thanksgiving for the gift of your Son, Jesus, who sets us free. As all in heaven bow down and worship before you, so may we acknowledge your kingdom this day through our praise. You live and reign as one God—Father, Son, and Holy Spirit—forever and ever. Amen.

Thursday of the Fifth Week of Lent

Scriptures
Genesis 17:3–9;
John 8:51–59

Hymn
And when from death I'm free, I'll sing on, I'll sing on;
And when from death I'm free, I'll sing on;

Overcome with Paschal Joy

And when from death I'm free, I'll sing and joyful be,
And through eternity I'll sing on, I'll sing on!
And through eternity I'll sing on.

"WHAT WONDROUS LOVE IS THIS?" VERSE 3

Reflection: Just like the third verse of "What Wondrous Love Is This?" is about singing on after death, so are today's biblical texts all about singing on after death. God promises Abram that he will become the father of a host of nations and maintain the covenant with Abram's descendants long after Abram is dead. Furthermore, God promises to give the land to which Abram has migrated as a permanent possession. Thus, Abram's descendants will sing on long after Abram's death.

The Johannine Jesus tells his Jewish adversaries that if they keep his word, they will never see death. Of course, they know that this is impossible. Even Abraham died. The prophets died. Jesus informs those listening to him that Abraham rejoiced to see his day. In other words, Abraham keeps singing on! This gives Jesus the opportunity to declare that before Abraham came to be, he existed. The Jews pick up stones to throw at him, but he disappears.

We live in a death-denying and death-defying culture. In our world, people do not die; they merely pass or pass away. People seldom die at home with their family members surrounding them; they die in sterile hospitals or in nursing homes. Medicine has been given the task to defy death with treatments, surgeries, and drugs. The Christian, while he or she preserves life, does not get involved in all the death-denying and death-defying practices. The Christian is set free by death to sing God's praises eternally.

Meditation
What death-denying and death-defying values
have you absorbed from the culture?
How does your Christian faith address those?

Fifth Week of Lent

Prayer

Even though your servant Abram was as good as dead, almighty God, your promised him countless descendants to sing your praise. After your own Son was dead on the cross, you raised him to newness of life. Give us the faith and strength to resist whatever gets in our way of coming to you and singing your praises for all eternity. You are one God—Father, Son, and Holy Spirit—forever and ever. Amen.

Friday of the Fifth Week of Lent

Scriptures
Jeremiah 20:10–13;
John 10:31–42

Hymn

What wondrous love is this, O my soul, O my soul!?
What wondrous love is this, O my soul!?
What wondrous love is this
That caused the Lord of bliss
To bear the dreadful curse for my soul, for my soul;
To bear the dreadful curse for my soul?

"WHAT WONDROUS LOVE IS THIS?" VERSE 1

Reflection: Verse one of "What Wondrous Love Is This?" is all about Jesus bearing the dreadful curse of Adam. We must remember that Adam and Eve were cursed by God with hard work and child-bearing and thrown out of the garden. In popular understanding, Jesus bore that curse to the cross and made amends for the first couple's trespasses. The singer of the first verse of the hymn understands this to be a wondrous love that caused Jesus to suffer and die for his soul.

Biblical cursing is not about saying bad or four-letter words. Biblical cursing is wishing evil upon another, like God wishes evil upon Adam and Eve. The prophet Jeremiah records another type of cursing. His enemies are whispering denunciations behind his back, because Jeremiah keeps telling

Overcome with Paschal Joy

both rulers and people what they need to do. They look for a way to trap him, so that they can shame him and get rid of him.

Jesus is being cursed by the Jews in John's Gospel. They have picked up rocks to stone him because they accuse him of blasphemy, making himself God. Jesus does not curse them in return; he attempts to convince them that God has sent him into the world to perform the Father's works; he is in the Father and the Father is in him. They only attempt to curse him more and to arrest him, but he flees across the Jordan from their power. In just a few days, Jesus will demonstrate the wondrous love that he shares with the Father through his death on the cross, a death that removes the ancient curse.

Meditation
What work has God wrought in your life
that demonstrates his wondrous love?

Prayer
Almighty LORD, you displayed your wondrous love for all people on the cross of your Son. After he undone the dreadful curse, your raised him to eternal life. Make us so grateful for this great gift that we praise you, Father, Son, and Holy Spirit, now and forever and ever. Amen.

Saturday of the Fifth Week of Lent

Scriptures
Ezekiel 37:21–28;
John 11:45–56

Hymn
Christ Jesus, we adore you,
Our thorn-crowned Lord and King.
We bow our hearts before you,
And to your Cross we cling.
Lord, give us strength to bear it
With patience and with love,

Fifth Week of Lent

That we may truly merit
A glorious crown above.

"O SACRED HEAD, SURROUNDED," VERSE 3

Reflection: In the passage from Ezekiel, the prophet records the Lord GOD declaring that he will gather from captivity and bring back to the promised land his chosen people, making them into one nation and establishing someone from the line of David to rule them. They will no longer defile themselves with idol worship. And God will renew his everlasting covenant with them; he will dwell with them. He will be their God, and they will be his people.

The promise that his people will never again become two kingdoms, but will be united as one under a Davidic descendant is the reason that passage from Ezekiel is paired with the passage from John's Gospel. After realizing the problem Jesus has caused for the high priest and the Pharisees, they meet to decide what must be done about him. The high priest Caiaphas proposes the solution that it would be better for one man to die for the people than for the people to die because they believe in him and cause social unrest that sparks Roman crackdown. The author of John's Gospel knows that Caiaphas' statement can be understood in two ways. It can refer to the situation literally as described above. It can also refer to the fact that Jesus would die not only for the Jewish nation, but for all nations.

The passage ends with the author's note that Passover was near. In John's Gospel, Jesus dies at the same time as the lambs are being slaughtered in the temple in preparation to celebrate Passover. After being crowned with thorns, he carries his cross with patience and love and finishes the work entrusted to him by the Father. Thus, he fulfills Caiaphas' words: He dies for the nation of the Jews and the nations of the Gentiles.

Meditation
What does it mean to you to say that Jesus died for you?

Prayer
Christ Jesus, we adore you and we bow our hearts before your cross. Give us the strength to carry our own crosses in imitation of you. And just as the Father

raised you to new life, grant that we may truly merit a glorious crown with you and the Father and the Holy Spirit forever and ever. Amen.

7

Holy Week

Palm Sunday of the Passion of the Lord, Cycle A

Scriptures
Matthew 21:1–11;
Isaiah 50:4–7;
Philippians 2:6–11;
Matthew 26:14–27:66

Hymn
All glory, praise, and honor
To you, Redeemer, King!
To whom the lips of children
Made sweet hosannas ring.
You are the King of Israel
And David's royal son,
Now in the Lord's Name coming,
Our King and Blessed One.

"ALL GLORY, PRAISE, AND HONOR," REFRAIN AND VERSE 1

Reflection: The first verse of "All Glory, Praise, and Honor" captures the essence of Matthew's narrative about Jesus' entry into Jerusalem from the

Overcome with Paschal Joy

Mount of Olives on a donkey and her colt. Some people miss this unique point in the First Gospel's account. Most likely, the author has misremembered his source, Zechariah 9:9. It would be impossible for Jesus to ride a donkey and her colt at the same time! Nevertheless, the refrain and verse one of "All Glory, Praise, and Honor" echoes the cry of the crowds: "Hosanna to the Son of David! Blessed is the one who comes in the name of the Lord! Hosanna in the highest heaven!" (Matt 21:9)

The triumphal procession's refrain quickly becomes, "Let him be crucified!" (Matt 27:22b, 23b) Matthew's account of Jesus' handing over and death are etched with the theme of betrayal more than any other gospel account. Judas, whose name is usually associated with the word "betrayal," is not the only betrayer in Matthew's story. However, Judas does betray Jesus for thirty pieces of silver, but, then, unique to this account is the fact that Judas betrays himself by committing suicide. Judas is contrasted with Peter, who also betrays Jesus three times; however, rather than despairing, he repents and weeps bitterly.

The crowds betray Jesus. They had welcomed him with "Hosanna," which means "Save us." However, in order to be politically correct, they follow the lead of their authorities—both religious and secular—and chant their death wish. Even Pilate is a betrayer, uniquely washing his hands of Jesus' blood, even though he found him innocent of any crime, and then handing him over to be crucified.

In Matthew's Gospel, even Jesus thinks that God has betrayed him. His last words, "My God, my God, why have you forsaken me?" (Matt 27:46) echo the betrayal theme that Matthew has woven through this text. We know that God has not betrayed his Son, because we know how the story ends. God raised Jesus from the dead. And that is the lesson we need to learn on this Palm Sunday of the Passion of the Lord. When we have been betrayed by spouse, family, or friends, we can find comfort in the One who was betrayed for us. We may hear "Hosanna" ("Good Job") first, but "Let him or her be crucified" ("Fire him," "Fire her," "Make it hard for him or her") may follow thereafter.

Meditation
When have you been betrayed by another? Who was the betrayer?
Did he or she repent? And did you forgive him or her?

Holy Week

Prayer

All glory, praise, and honor to you, Jesus Christ, our Redeemer and King. As we sing "Hosanna" to you this day, King of Israel, guard us from all harm and keep us from betraying those we love. Grant us the grace to follow you, David's royal son, through death to new life. You are the Blessed One, living and reigning with the Father and the Holy Spirit forever and ever. Amen.

Palm Sunday of the Passion of the Lord, Cycle B

Scriptures

Mark 11:1–10 or John 12:12–16;
Isaiah 50:4–7;
Philippians 2:6–11;
Mark 14:1–15:47

Hymn

All glory, praise, and honor
To you, Redeemer, King!
To whom the lips of children
Made sweet hosannas ring.
The company of angels
Are praising you on high;
And mortals joined with all things
Created, make reply.

"ALL GLORY, PRAISE, AND HONOR," REFRAIN AND VERSE 2

Reflection: The account of Jesus' suffering and death in Mark's Gospel, considered to be the oldest among the four gospels, is filled with the theme of abandonment. The reader is introduced to this theme in Jesus' first public act of calling disciples in Mark's Gospel. First, he calls Peter and Andrew, who abandon their boat and follow him. Then, he calls James and John, who abandon their father and follow him. Since this is the author's favorite theme, we should expect to find it in his account of Jesus' suffering and death.

Overcome with Paschal Joy

First, Jesus is abandoned by his disciple named Judas, who once he has identified Jesus with a kiss, disappears from the story, never to be heard of again. Jesus is abandoned by Peter, James, and John, who cannot stay awake. He is abandoned by all his followers; once he is arrested, they leave him and flee. Unique to Mark's Gospel is the young man with a linen cloth wrapped around him, who also abandons Jesus and runs away naked. Peter, who follows Jesus at a distance, abandons him three times to the high priest's maids.

Second, the crowds abandon Jesus. A few days before, they had shouted, "Hosanna!" Now, they shout "Crucify him!" Pilate, wishing to satisfy the crowds, abandons Jesus to death. Even Jesus thinks that God has abandoned him, making his last words, "My God, my God, why have you forsaken me?" (Mark 15:34) After Jesus dies, he is buried, and three days later some women find his tomb open and his body missing, but they say nothing to anyone. And thus ends the abandonment theme in Mark's Gospel!

Not only were the original, intended readers experiencing abandonment at the time of the writing of this account (cf. Mark 13:12), but abandonment is a universal theme. This means that it can be found in the lives of most people around the world. Parents abandon children on streets, in orphanages, in cars, and to death. Employers abandon faithful employees to wage cuts and firing. Older children run away from home and abandon their parents. We do not like to dwell on this abandonment theme, but it can be found in the fiber of our being. Mark chose to reveal it in the life of Jesus; we can find it in our own lives if we look carefully.

Meditation
What types of abandonment have you experienced?
How do those help you understand the theme of abandonment
in Mark's passion account?

Prayer
All glory, praise, and honor to you, Redeemer and King, who was abandoned to the cross by those you loved. Through your resurrection from the dead, you have revealed the truth that out of abandonment there comes new and exciting life. Let my mortal praise this day join that of the angels in heaven who adore you now and forever and ever. Amen.

Holy Week

Palm Sunday of the Passion of the Lord, Cycle C

Scriptures
Luke 19:28–40;
Isaiah 50:4–7;
Philippians 2:6–11;
Luke 22:14–23:56

Hymn
All glory, praise, and honor
To you, Redeemer, King!
To whom the lips of children
Made sweet hosannas ring.
The people of the Hebrews
With palms before you went;
Our praise and prayers and anthems
Before you we present.

"ALL GLORY, PRAISE, AND HONOR," REFRAIN AND VERSE 3

Reflection: Because the author of Luke's Gospel is a master storyteller, he likes to echo themes and lines in later parts of his work that he used in earlier parts of his narrative in order to make connections for his readers. This written technique is similar to the flashback technique used in film; a connection between an earlier event and a later event in a story are recalled by the director for the viewer.

As Jesus rides into Jerusalem on a donkey, the crowds proclaiming him sing, "Peace in heaven, and glory in the highest heaven!" (Luke 19:38b) This line is meant to echo the angels' song at Jesus' birth: "Glory to God in the highest heaven, and on earth peace among those whom he favors!" (Luke 2:14) These peaceful songs prepare the reader for Luke's long passion account and his unique theme of Jesus' innocence. In other words, almost everyone in Luke's Gospel thinks that Jesus is innocent of any crime.

First, Pilate declares Jesus innocent; he finds no guilt in him. Second, Pilate sends Jesus to Herod, who returns him to Pilate with a decree of innocence, that is, not guilty of any capital crime. Third, once Jesus is crucified, one of the other two men crucified with him—who have speaking parts in Luke's Gospel—declares Jesus to be innocent. Fourth, Jesus innocently places himself in his Father's hands, declaring, "Father, into your hands I commend my spirit" (Luke 23:46), only to be followed by the centurion's words: "Certainly, this man was innocent" (Luke 23:47).

In Luke's Gospel, Jesus dies the death of a martyr in order to serve as a model for those who were dying the same type of death near the end of the first century. The model is repeated in Luke's second volume, the Acts of the Apostles, in the person of the deacon Stephen, who recites the same lines as Jesus before he is stoned to death. While we may think that martyrdom is a thing of the early church, many people die a martyr's death today either literally or metaphorically for their faith and the principles upon which they stand. The palm branches carried today represent our willingness to be martyrs, like those whose images we see in stained glass windows grasping a palm branch in their hands.

Meditation
When have you metaphorically been martyred?
Look through a magazine, newspaper, or search the internet
for a recent story about the martyrdom of a believer.
What do you learn from the story?

Prayer
The Hebrews greeted you, Lord Jesus, with palms of martyrdom. Hear our praises, prayers, and anthems that we present to you and make us worthy to bear the name Christian. May all glory, praise, and honor be yours in union with the Father and the Holy Spirit, one God, forever and ever. Amen.

Monday of Holy Week

Scriptures
Isaiah 42:1-7;
John 12:1-11

Holy Week

Hymn
And that a higher gift than grace
Should flesh and blood refine,
God's presence and his very self,
And essence all divine.

"PRAISE TO THE HOLIEST IN THE HEIGHT," VERSE 4

Reflection: The fourth verse of "Praise to the Holiest in the Height" and the Scripture texts assigned for this Monday of Holy Week emphasize the servant nature of Jesus. In his first oracle about the servant of the LORD, Isaiah writes about the servant whom God upholds, the chosen one with whom he is pleased. This servant receives the LORD's Spirit so that he can bring justice to the nations of the world. Isaiah's description of God's servant is applied to God's Son.

Mary is portrayed as a servant in John's Gospel. Mary, sister of Lazarus and Martha, anoints Jesus' feet with a bottle of costly aromatic nard. This sparks Judas the Iscariot to declare that the perfumed oil could have been sold for a year's wage and the money given to the poor. Jesus' response to Judas is very simple. Mary has prepared him for burial. The poor will be around even after he is dead and raised. She has served him now.

The fourth verse of "Praise to the Holiest in the Height" further develops the servant concept. The LORD offered the gift of himself, grace, to people. However, in the person of the flesh and blood of Jesus, God's divine essence dwelt. Jesus was God in human form among human beings. And just as he, divine, served both his Father and others, we find in him a model of the servanthood that should characterize his followers.

Meditation
What aspects of servant best characterize your life?
Which of those aspects do you find in the life of Jesus?

Prayer
LORD God, you created the heaves and stretched them out; you spread the earth with its crops; you give breath to people and spirit to those who walk on

it. Help me to follow the example of Jesus, your servant and your Son, that I may faithfully serve you and others all my days. I ask this through the same Jesus Christ, who lives and reigns with you and the Holy Spirit, one God, forever and ever. Amen.

Tuesday of Holy Week

Scriptures
Isaiah 49:1–6;
John 13:21–33, 36–38

Hymn
O gen'rous love! that he who smote
In man for man the foe,
The double agony in man
For man should undergo.

"PRAISE TO THE HOLIEST IN THE HEIGHT," VERSE 5

Reflection: The "he" in verse five of "Praise to the Holiest in the Height" refers to Jesus, whose generous love, manifested in the cross, smote evil for people. In other words, Jesus the man defeated evil for people by undergoing it. He defeated death by dying; that is the "double agony" mentioned in the verse above, and that is also the oxymoronic truth presented in the Scripture texts on this Tuesday of Holy Week.

Isaiah's second oracle about the servant of the LORD tells about one called by name from birth and made into a sharp-edged sword and polished arrow to effectively bring God's word to his people. The servant is like a light to all nations so that the LORD's salvation can reach to the ends of the earth. Judas is not the servant Isaiah describes; he is interested only in himself. The author of John's Gospel clearly states that Jesus identifies him to the beloved disciple with a morsel of food dipped into a common dish. Judas is no light, as he leaves the gathering at night.

Once the darkness is gone, Jesus, God's servant, can declare that God will glorify him soon. Jesus is the light of the world, and those who follow him walk in that light. That is how others can tell if one is a servant of God; the servant spreads light through his or her way of life. The pretend servant, like Judas, spreads darkness.

Meditation
What light shines from you? How does that light glorify God?

Prayer
Generous Father, even more generous was your Son. Through his death and resurrection, he defeated death and made it possible for me to hope for new life on the other side of death. As I remember his passion this Holy Week, turn my good deeds into light that they may glorify you, who live and reign with Jesus Christ and the Holy Spirit, forever and ever. Amen.

Wednesday of Holy Week

Scriptures
Isaiah 50:4–9a;
Matthew 26:14–25

Hymn
All glory, praise, and honor
To you, Redeemer, King!
To whom the lips of children
Made sweet hosannas ring.
To you before your passion
They sang their hymns of praise.
To you, now high exalted,
Our melody we raise.

"ALL GLORY, PRAISE, AND HONOR," REFRAIN AND VERSE 4

Overcome with Paschal Joy

Reflection: It is easy during Holy Week to think that we are re-enacting the last days of Jesus' life. After all, we take the parts of the gospel on Palm Sunday of the Passion of the Lord, we mark his last supper on Holy Thursday, and we venerate his cross on Good Friday. However, these are remembrances, not re-enactments. We remember what happened to Jesus, and, through reflection on these events, we discover how the same things are happening to us. Thus, as the fourth verse of the "All Glory, Praise, and Honor" states, just as the Jews sang hymns of praise before Jesus' passion, now we raise melodies to him as the highly exalted or resurrected One.

Like the servant in Isaiah's third oracle, Jesus embraces his Father's will and prepares to move forward to accomplish it. He has spoken the Father's word to people. He has not rebelled or turned away when some would not listen to him. Even acknowledging his betrayer does not stop him from his assigned task. He moves forward, knowing that God is with him.

We remember Jesus' determination and reflect upon our own. When the going gets tough, it is easy to stop. God's agenda can quickly give way to our own. We may even discover ourselves in rebellion. A friend used to ask: When a person and God get in a fight, who will win? Faithfulness has to be strong even when we know that some will not listen, even when we know that some will rebel, even when we know our betrayer. Throughout the Bible, God moves forward, and so should we.

Meditation

During this Holy Week, what event that occurred to Jesus do you remember? How do you see that event present in your life now?

Prayer

Father of our Lord Jesus Christ, you heard the prayer of your Son during his passion, and in your great love you answered him by giving him strength to accomplish your will. Hear the prayers I bring before you and strengthen me in your service. All glory, praise, and honor be yours, now and forever. Amen.

The Paschal Triduum

Thursday of the Lord's Supper: Holy Thursday

Scriptures
Exodus 12:1–8, 11–14;
1 Corinthians 11:23–26;
John 13:1–15

Hymn
At the Lamb's high feast we sing
Praise to our victorious King.
He has washed us in the tide
Flowing from his wounded side.
Praise the Lord, whose love divine
Gives his sacred blood for wine,
Give his body for the feast,
Christ the victim, Christ the priest.

"AT THE LAMB'S HIGH FEAST WE SING," VERSE 1

Reflection: When the Evening Mass of the Lord's Supper begins, Lent ends. The purpose of Lent is to prepare to celebrate The Sacred Paschal Triduum, which begins with the Mass of the Lord's Supper on Holy Thursday and ends with Evening Prayer on Easter Sunday. Verse one of "At the Lamb's High Feast We Sing" incorporates the themes woven into this once-a-year celebration of the Lamb, whose blood on the doorposts and lintel of every

Overcome with Paschal Joy

Hebrew home saved the people from death. In John's Gospel, the Lamb washes the feet of his disciples and institutes the church from his side as blood (eucharist) and water (baptism) flow forth.

One of the foci of the Mass of the Lord's Supper is the gift of the eucharist, which flows from the wounded side of Jesus on the cross and is attested to by St. Paul in his First Letter to the Corinthians. Paul narrates how he is handing on to the believers in Corinth what he received, namely, that Jesus gave his body as bread and his blood as wine to his followers before he died. They continue to remember this gift, proclaiming his death until he comes again. Christ is both the victim offered and the priest who offers himself to God. Christ is the sacrificial victim who dies no more, the Lamb, once slain, who lives forever. He is the priest, the altar, and the Lamb of sacrifice.

The washing of the feet of twelve people is not merely a re-enactment of Jesus' unique Johannine action of washing the feet of his disciples. It is eucharist in action. Offering a donation in the name of a runner or cyclist who is raising funds for a worthy cause is eucharist in action. Volunteering in the local soup kitchen is eucharist in action. Serving in the food pantry or in the homeless shelter is eucharist in action. There is more to eucharist than just drinking the sacred blood as wine or receiving the sacred body in the feast; eucharist requires some form of ministry that reaches outward to others, drawing them in to the Lamb's high feast.

So, on this Holy Thursday, we mark the high feast of the Lamb of God, and we praise him for his victory over sin and death. He has washed us in the baptismal tide that flows from his wounded side, just as the lamb's blood of old washed away death for the Hebrews. Jesus' divine love was so great that he continues to give his body and blood under the forms of bread and wine as nourishment for our journey through life. Thus, Christ is the victim offered, the priest who offers himself, and the altar upon whom the offering is made. Our praise this day spurs us to take this active gift to the whole world.

Meditation
In what specific ways do you take eucharist into the world?
In what specific ways do you turn eucharist into active ministry?

The Paschal Triduum

Prayer

At this high feast of your Son, O LORD, we sing to you. We praise you for Jesus' death and resurrection that has washed us clean and that nourishes us with his body and his blood. As we celebrate so great a gift, we offer in thanksgiving the Lamb who is both victim and priest. Grant that through this feast we may overflow in charity. We ask this through the same Jesus Christ, your Son, who lives and reigns with you and the Holy Spirit, one God, forever and ever. Amen.

Friday of the Passion of the Lord: Good Friday

Scriptures
Isaiah 52:13–53:12;
Hebrews 4:14–16; 5:7–9;
John 18:1–19:42

Hymn
Were you there when they nailed him to the tree?
Were you there when they nailed him to the tree?
O sometimes it causes me to tremble, tremble, tremble;
Were you there when they nailed him to the tree?

"WERE YOU THERE WHEN THEY CRUCIFIED MY LORD?" VERSE 2

Reflection: While there are many images presented to us on Good Friday, the cross is the predominate one. Isaiah's fourth and final oracle about the servant of the Lord—especially his marred human appearance, a man of suffering, pierced and crushed, like a lamb led to the slaughter, etc.—prepares for the Johannine account of Jesus' glorious suffering, death, and resurrection. In John's Gospel, Jesus is in charge of everything that happens to him! He identifies himself as I AM, that is, God, to those who come to arrest him in the garden; he declares his kingship not of this world to Pilate and dialogues with the governor about the source of his power; he carries the cross by himself; he entrusts the care of his mother to the beloved disciple; from his wounded side he gives birth to the church with water (baptism) and blood (eucharist); and he is buried in a garden to indicate that new life is already stirring his dead corpse. In the center of all these actions is the cross.

Because John's Gospel glorifies the cross, it is necessary that we reclaim it for the instrument of capital punishment that it was in the ancient world. The Romans used it to intimidate conquered peoples into submission to Roman authority and government. Roman citizens were exempt from this form of death. That is why on this Good Friday we need to venerate the cross; we need to come forward and touch its rough wood, feel the splinters with our lips, or bow before its huge presence. In our modern world, the cross has been turned to silver and gold and cleaned up. Good Friday is meant to get us back in touch with the horror of this ancient means of capital punishment.

After reading and/or participating in the glorious passion account of John's Gospel and after venerating the cross, we can answer "Yes" to the question posed by the second verse of "Were You There When They Crucified My Lord?": "Were you there when they nailed him to the tree?" We were there because we continue to eat of the fruit of the tree of life which bore the savior of the world; we eat his body and drink his blood. We were there because we continue to live in the redeemed garden of the world in which began his saving passion and in which his dead body was quickened with new life; we have been baptized into his death and resurrection. Knowing either of these answers should cause us to tremble, tremble, tremble!

Meditation

What causes you to tremble when venerating the cross of Christ?

Prayer

Father of our Lord Jesus Christ, you made the tree of defeat of Adam and Eve the tree of victory of your Son. Even as he hung on the cross, drained of water and blood, you quickened life in him. Keep us faithful to him, who lives and reigns with you and the Holy Spirit, one God, forever and ever. Amen.

The Paschal Triduum

The Easter Vigil in the Holy Night: Holy Saturday

Scriptures
Genesis 1:1–2:2; Genesis 22:1–18;
Exodus 14:15–15:1; Isaiah 54:5–14;
Isaiah 55:1–11; Baruch 3:9–15, 32–4:4;
Ezekiel 36:16–17a, 18–28; Romans 6:3–11;
Matthew 28:1–10 (Cycle A), Mark 16:1–7 (Cycle B),
Luke 24:1-12 (Cycle C)

Hymn
Were you there when he rose from out the tomb?
Were you there when he rose from out the tomb?
O sometimes it causes me to tremble, tremble, tremble;
Were you there when he rose from out the tomb?

"WERE YOU THERE WHEN THEY CRUCIFIED MY LORD?" VERSE 6

Reflection: The Easter Vigil oozes with new life. It begins with the new life of the new fire kindled outside the church. That new life and fire is brought inside as a single flame atop the Paschal Candle, representing Christ risen from the dead, then it is shared by every baptized person who holds an unlit taper. New life spreads like a wild fire through the assembly!

New life is found in some form in all the Scripture texts assigned to this holy night. God creates the first new life. Once Abraham passes the LORD's test, he receives the new life of Isaac, who was as good as dead. The Hebrews, dead in slavery, march through the Sea of Reeds to find new life on the other side. The LORD, Israel's God, keeps calling his people to new covenant life. Those who are thirsty are invited to come to the water. Those who seek knowledge are invited to come to the source of all wisdom. Those exiled in Babylon are promised new life through sprinkling with water. And those who are baptized into Christ die and rise with him to new life.

This enervating newness is because of the empty tomb discovered by Mary Magdalene and another Mary in Matthew's Gospel; by Mary Magdalene, Mary, the mother of James, and Salome in Mark's Gospel' and Mary Magdalene, Joanna, and Mary the mother of James in Luke's Gospel. It makes no difference if there is a great earthquake and an angel descends from heaven and rolls back the stone sealing the entrance to the tomb (Matthew's Gospel), or if the women find the stone already rolled back and a young man sitting in the tomb (Mark's Gospel), or if the women find the stone already rolled back and two men in dazzling garments appear (Luke's Gospel). None of these details matter because the focus is on the new life that emerges from the grave of death!

In answer to the question posed by verse six of "Were You There When They Crucified My Lord?" namely, "Were you there when he rose from out the tomb?" we can shout, "Yes!" All the new life that has stirred in us because of prayer, fasting, and almsgiving is a taste of the new life that awaits us on the other side of death. All of the re-creating that God has done in us, all of God's tests that we have passed, all the passages that we have made through the seas of change and chaos, all the thirst for the Divine that we have felt, all the heavenly wisdom that we have sought, all the times that we have been sprinkled clean with forgiveness—all these and more are experiences of new life oozing out of us. All we can do at the end of this holy night is shout, "Alleluia!"

Meditation
What specific new life is stirring in you this Holy Saturday?

Prayer
The earth overflows with your goodness, O LORD. You have sent forth your Spirit and renewed the earth and every living creature and thing upon it. Through the resurrection of your Son, you have satisfied our thirst and given us a spring of salvation. Draw us ever deeper into the new life you revealed through the empty tomb, and grant that we may one day share fully in it with Jesus Christ and the Holy Spirit, who live and reign with you, Father, forever and ever. Amen. Alleluia!

8

First Week of Easter

Easter Sunday of the Resurrection of the Lord, Cycles A, B, and C

Scriptures
Acts 10:34a, 37–43;
Colossians 3:1–4 or 1 Corinthians 5:6b–8;
John 20:1–9

Hymn
Alleluia, alleluia, alleluia.
O sons and daughters let us sing!
The King of heav'n, the glorious King,
O'er death today rose triumphing. Alleluia!

"O SONS AND DAUGHTERS," REFRAIN AND VERSE 1

Reflection: We must remember that in John's Gospel, Jesus' tomb is located in a garden. And all kinds of things can happen in a garden! Mary Magdalene alone goes to the tomb while it is still dark and sees the stone removed from the tomb. Her first response is to run and tell Simon Peter and the beloved disciple that someone has taken the body of Jesus from the tomb in the dark of night. See, Mary Magdalene is still in the dark; she does not yet believe in the resurrection. Likewise, Simon Peter looks into the dark tomb and does not yet believe. However, the beloved disciple emerges from the dark tomb into the light of the early morning, sees, and believes. Anything can happen in a garden!

In his First Letter to the Corinthians, Paul prefers the yeast metaphor to the garden metaphor. Everyone who has ever made and baked a loaf of bread knows that a little yeast causes the whole batch of dough to rise. Jesus is the little yeast, leavening everyone who comes in contact with him. St. Paul then changes the metaphor to the paschal lamb; Christ, the new paschal lamb, has been sacrificed states the apostle. Today, we celebrate the feast of him who died like a lamb and rose like a loaf of bread. According to the letter to the Colossians, he is now seated at God's right hand from where he will one day appear in glory.

Easter Sunday has a variety of satellite images associated with the new life that emerges from death's tomb that appeal to all the senses. The Easter egg, itself a tomb, turns into a chick once it is incubated. The prolific rabbit is an image of abundant life over and over again. And the traditional Easter basket, filled with sweets and treats, activates the nose and taste buds with new life. On Easter Sunday we cannot help but sing "Alleluia" to Christ the glorious king, who, today, over death rose triumphing!

Meditation

What is your favorite image associated with Easter Sunday?
How does it capture the essence of Easter for you?

Prayer

We give thanks to you, O Father, for your mercy that endures forever. With your right hand you rolled away the stone protecting the dead body of your Son and raised him to new life. As we keep this festival in his honor, make us aware of the many blessings with which you have graced us, and grant that on the day of death we may be raised to life with Christ, who lives and reigns with you and the Holy Spirit, one God, forever and ever. Amen. Alleluia!

First Week of Easter

Monday within the Octave of Easter

Scriptures
Acts 2:14, 22–33;
Matthew 28:8–15

Hymn
Alleluia, alleluia, alleluia.
An angel clad in white they see,
Who sat and spoke unto the three,
"Your Lord has gone to Galilee." Alleluia!

"O SONS AND DAUGHTERS," REFRAIN AND VERSE 3

Reflection: The third verse from "O Sons and Daughters" reflects the version of the empty tomb story found in Matthew's Gospel. After an earthquake, an angel, robed in white, descends from heaven and rolls away the stone from the tomb, revealing to Mary Magdalene and another Mary the emptiness of the grave. Today's passage from Matthew's Gospel continues the account. Jesus appears to the women as they leave the tomb, and he commissions them to go tell his disciples that he is going to Galilee, where they will see him.

In one of many of Peter's speeches in the Acts of the Apostles, the first among the apostles rehearses some of the events that led to God's raising of Jesus from the throes of death. Speaking on behalf of the rest of the disciples, Peter declares that they are witnesses to the resurrection. A witness is one who testifies to the truth; so, while standing before the Jews, Peter declares that Jesus the Nazorean was a man commended to them by God with mighty deeds, wonders, and signs, which God worked through him in their midst. Peter's words about mighty deeds, wonders, and signs echo the account of the exodus as the LORD led the Israelites from slavery to freedom through the Sea of Reeds and gave them water to drink from the rock and manna to eat from the sky.

According to Peter's Pentecost speech, those mighty deeds, wonders, and signs were present in the life of Jesus of Nazareth. And this should be enough for people to believe that he was one of God's chosen ones. Because experience dictates that once a person has died he or she has a tendency to remain dead, this is extraordinary preaching on Peter's part and extraordinary faith on the part of those who believe that God has done another mighty deed at which people can wonder and, hopefully, understand the meaning of the sign of the empty tomb.

Meditation
What do you consider to be God's greatest mighty deed, wonder, or sign in your life?

Prayer
Ever-living God, our hearts are glad and our souls rejoice to celebrate the resurrection of your Son from the dead. You did not abandon him to the nether world, nor did you suffer him to undergo corruption. With the gift of the Holy Spirit strengthen our faith in the new life you have lavished on the world and bring us to its fullness in the kingdom of heaven. We ask this through the same Jesus Christ, who with you and the Holy Spirit are one God, forever and ever. Amen. Alleluia!

Tuesday within the Octave of Easter

Scriptures
Acts 2:36–41;
John 20:11-18

Hymn
Alleluia, alleluia, alleluia.
That Easter morn, at break of day,
The faithful women went their way
To seek the tomb where Jesus lay. Alleluia!
"O SONS AND DAUGHTERS," REFRAIN AND VERSE 2

Reflection: In John's Gospel, after Mary Magdalene discovers the empty tomb and tells Simon Peter and the beloved disciple, who run to the tomb to verify Mary's report, she returns to the tomb, sees two angels in it, and explains that Jesus' body has been taken. Not recognizing Jesus standing beside her and thinking that he was the gardener—remember, the Gospel of John is specific about the tomb being in a garden—Mary requests the body. When Jesus pronounces her name, immediately she recognizes him and attempts to hug him. He sends her to his disciples with a message, which she delivers to them.

It is from this account in John's Gospel that Mary Magdalene is known as the apostle to the apostles. The word "apostle" means "one who is sent." The risen Christ sends Mary to his disciples. Thus, she is a female apostle to whom the message of resurrection has been entrusted. She makes certain that Jesus' followers know that God has made the crucified Jesus both Lord, that is, Master, and Christ, that is, Anointed.

Faithful women, like Mary Magdalene, populate Christian history. Biblically, they lead small Christian communities. They build hospitals and orphanages to care for the sick and provide families for those who have none. They open schools and teach the illiterate. They march for basic human rights, like life, fair wages, and justice. And they are led by Mary Magdalene seeking the new life that emerges from the tomb in which Jesus' body was placed after he was crucified.

Meditation
Who was the most important Christian woman in your life?
What message did she deliver to you?

Prayer
On Easter morning, LORD, Mary Magdalene went to the tomb in the garden and discovered there your risen Son. Keep us faithful to her mission that we may never cease to proclaim his resurrection from the dead. He is Lord and Christ forever and ever. Amen. Alleluia!

Overcome with Paschal Joy

Wednesday within the Octave of Easter

Scriptures
Acts 3:1–10;
Luke 24:13–35

Hymn
Alleluia, alleluia, alleluia.
That night th' apostles met in fear;
Among them came their Lord most dear,
And said, "My peace be with you here." Alleluia!

"O SONS AND DAUGHTERS," REFRAIN AND VERSE 4

Reflection: Only Luke's Gospel contains the account of two of Jesus' disciples making a journey from Jerusalem to Emmaus on Easter Sunday evening. The astute reader will recognize immediately that the story is incomplete because it needs a third person. And so in the course of their walking, a stranger joins the two; now there are three, and a theophany can occur. A theophany, a manifestation of the Divine in some way—such as water, fire, light—occurs when the risen Christ takes bread, says the blessing, breaks it, and gives it to them. Their eyes are opened, they recognize him, and he vanishes from their sight. Such is the process of most theophanies. The two disciples have no choice except to head back to Jerusalem. Their hearts are burning, and they must tell the others what they have experienced. They find the others gathered together in fear. They challenge that fear with their message of resurrection only to hear from the others that Jesus has been raised and appeared to Simon Peter. Later that night, Jesus will appear to all of them and offer them his peace.

The journey theme is also manifest in the trip that Peter and John make to the temple, where they find a man crippled from birth. They invite him to travel with them by restoring his legs and feet in the name of Jesus Christ. The man is raised by Peter, and his feet and ankles grow strong. He leaps up, stands, and walks around, journeying with Peter and John into the temple.

First Week of Easter

While it is a trite and overused metaphor, life is a journey, and the Christian life is a journey from one theophany to another. The theophanies keep us walking from one to the next unexpected one. Climbing a mountain, one can see a tiny tundra flower that has a growing season of 60 days and be captured by its beauty; that is a theophany. Standing on the seashore and listening to waves lap the sand while watching the sun sink over the horizon can lift a person out of himself or herself for the briefest moment; that is a theophany. Sitting at the table with family or friends and passing people through conversation the way one passes food is a theophany. In these and in many more ways, the divine breaks through and Christ's peace descends upon us like rain on dry ground.

Meditation
What theophany have you most recently experienced?

Prayer
We give thanks to you, O LORD, and we invoke your name as we sing your praise and proclaim your marvelous deeds. You made holy the journey of Abraham and Sarah, Jacob and Rachel and Leah, and Moses and Zipporah by revealing your presence to them. You have made our journeys holy by revealing the resurrected presence of your Son. Grant that we may follow him with undivided hearts throughout our lives and into the kingdom, where he is Lord forever and ever. Amen. Alleluia!

Thursday within the Octave of Easter

Scriptures
Acts 3:11–26;
Luke 24:35–48

Hymn
Alleluia, alleluia, alleluia.
How blest are they who have not seen,
And yet whose faith has constant been,
For they eternal life shall win. Alleluia!

Overcome with Paschal Joy

"O SONS AND DAUGHTERS," REFRAIN AND VERSE 8

Reflection: Is it possible to see eternal life? The eighth verse of "O Sons and Daughters" declares that those who keep constant faith will win eternal life. But, again, can it be seen? The Acts of the Apostles seems to think so. After Peter and John heal a man crippled from birth, they begin to explain to their listeners that they are seeing eternal life in the healed man. The unnamed man's faith in Jesus has made him strong and given him perfect health. That is a manifestation of eternal life.

The narrator of Luke's Gospel also thinks that one can see eternal life. Following the return of the two disciples to Jerusalem from Emmaus, the risen Jesus appears in the midst of all the gathered disciples and offers them his peace to calm their fears. He demonstrates that it is really he, that he is participating in eternal life. Then, he re-commissions them to preach repentance in his name to the whole world.

Many people project their experience of eternal life to the other side of the grave; it is something to be experienced later. However, according to the Bible, it can be seen—and experienced—now. Go to the hospital and watch doctors perform heart surgery on a patient, and you will see eternal life. Go to the rehab center and watch an amputee learn to walk, and you will see eternal life. Visit a neighbor's garden or take a walk through a farmer's field (with permission of course), marveling at what you find growing in the earth, and you will see eternal life. Eternal life is visible if we but recognize and gaze upon it.

Meditation
Where do you see eternal life?

Prayer
O LORD, our God, your name is wonderful in all the earth. You have made us little less than the angels and crowned us with glory, honor, and eternal life through the resurrection of your Son. Make us always grateful for these gifts. We ask this through our Lord Jesus Christ, your Son, who lives and reigns with you and the Holy Spirit, one God, forever and ever. Amen. Alleluia!

First Week of Easter

Friday within the Octave of Easter

Scriptures
Acts 4:1–12;
John 21:1–14

Hymn
Crown him the Lord of life,
Who triumphed o'er the grave,
And rose victorious in the strife
For those he came to save:
All hail, Redeemer, hail!
For you have died for me;
Your praise shall never, never fail
Throughout eternity.

"CROWN HIM WITH MANY CROWNS," VERSE 4

Reflection: During the Easter Season, the sentence "the stone that the builders rejected has become the chief cornerstone" from Psalm 118:22 is heard frequently in both Responsorial Psalms and in Scripture texts. Psalm 118:22 is a proverb stating that what is insignificant to people has become great through God's work. Probably it originally referred to the cornerstone or the capstone of the Temple or some other building project, but in the Christian Bible (New Testament) it was used to refer to the death and resurrection of Christ in Matthew's Gospel (cf. 21:42), in Romans (cf. 9:33), in 1 Peter (cf. 2:7), and in today's passage from the Acts of the Apostles (cf. 4:11). Jesus is the stone rejected by the Jewish builders; however, through his resurrection from the dead, he has become the cornerstone of the church.

This same proverb is manifest in a different manner in a unique story in John's Gospel. Seven—a perfect number, the sum of three (indicating the divine) and four (indicating the earth)—of Jesus' disciples are in a boat fishing on the Sea of Tiberias, but, as usual, they catch nothing. They do not recognize Jesus standing on the shore, but they obey him when he tells them to cast their net to the right side of the boat. Once they make a huge catch, they recognize him and go to shore, where he has already prepared a

Overcome with Paschal Joy

fire with fish cooking on it and bread. Another version of this story appears in Luke's Gospel at the call of Simon (cf. 5:1–11). The One who was rejected and crucified has been raised from the dead, and he is back teaching his followers how to fish.

The fourth verse of "Crown Him with Many Crowns" captures all this in song. Christ triumphed over the grave and rose victorious in the battle for those he came to save. He is the Lord of life, the stone rejected by the builders who has become the cornerstone. So, on this Friday in the Octave of Easter, we hail him as our redeemer. His death destroyed death. For this great gift all we can do is praise him for all eternity.

Meditation
To what other people or situations can you apply the sentence "the stone which the builders rejected has become the cornerstone"?

Prayer
We give thanks to you, LORD, for you are good and your mercy endures forever. When the builders rejected the stone you had chosen, you made it the cornerstone of your church. Your mighty deed is wonderful in our eyes; we are glad and rejoice in the name of Jesus Christ, your Son, who lives and reigns with you and the Holy Spirit, one God, forever and ever. Amen. Alleluia!

Saturday within the Octave of Easter

Scriptures
Acts 4:13–21;
Mark 16:9–15

Hymn
Alleluia, alleluia, alleluia.
On this most holy day of days,
To God your hearts and voices raise,
In laud, and jubilee, and praise. Alleluia!

"O SONS AND DAUGHTERS," REFRAIN AND VERSE 9

First Week of Easter

Reflection: Today is the seventh day in the octave of Easter. In the whole of the liturgical year, there are only two octaves or eight-day celebrations. The first begins with the Nativity of the Lord (Christmas, December 25) and ends with the Solemnity of Mary, the Holy Mother of God (January 1). The second begins with Easter Sunday of the Resurrection of the Lord and ends with the Second Sunday of Easter. Before zero was invented in the ninth century, the first number was one. Thus, counting from Easter Sunday (one) to the Second Sunday of Easter equals eight days (an octave). Each day within the octave is considered a solemnity outranking any other solemnity or feast that may occur on any day within the octave. In other words, every day within the octave of Easter is Easter Sunday. This is why the last or ninth verse of "O Sons and Daughters" is appropriate today. This seventh day within the Easter Octave is one of the most holy day of days, and we should raise our hearts and voices in laud, jubilee, and praise of God.

This is what Peter and John do in the Acts of the Apostles. They praise God for curing the lame man in the name of Jesus of Nazareth. Even though the Jewish leaders, elders, and scribes order Peter and John not to speak or teach in the name of Jesus, they make it very clear that it is impossible for them not to speak about what they have seen and heard. Like them, we should be heard lauding God for all the new life that he has lavished upon us.

The third ending of Mark's Gospel is presented as a summary of this week. Yes, Mark's Gospel has three endings: the original at 16:8; a shorter ending consisting of another sentence added to 16:8; and the third ending 16:9–20, from which today's passage is taken. The third ending is a summary of the endings of Matthew's Gospel and Luke's Gospel. It is chosen today because it sends us into the whole world to proclaim the gospel to every creature. In other words, it sends us into the world in laud, jubilee, and praise of God for the resurrection of Jesus Christ.

Meditation

What does the keeping of an octave in laud, jubilee, and praise of God mean to you?

Prayer

Father, we give thanks to you for your mercy, strength, and courage. Your right hand raised your Son from death and made him the Lord of all life. On this

Overcome with Paschal Joy

most holy day of days we raise our hearts and voices in laud, jubilee, and praise of you, your Son, Jesus Christ, and the Holy Spirit, living and reigning as one God, forever and ever. Amen. Alleluia!

9

Second Week of Easter

On Sundays during the Easter Season there are three entries, one each for Cycles A, B, and C, as noted in the introduction. Choose the one that corresponds to the current year's readings.

Second Sunday of Easter, Cycle A

Scriptures
Acts 2:42–47;
1 Peter 1:3–9;
John 20:19–31

Hymn
Alleluia, alleluia, alleluia.
When Thomas first the tidings heard,
How they had seen the risen Lord,
He doubted the disciples' word. Alleluia!

"O SONS AND DAUGHTERS," VERSE 5

Reflection: The fifth verse of "O Sons and Daughters" summarizes the story heard from John's Gospel on this octave—eighth day—of Easter. In John's Gospel, Jesus appears to the disciples by passing through the locked doors of the place where they are gathered on Easter Sunday evening. After wishing them peace, he breathes the Holy Spirit into them. One disciple, Thomas, is missing. So, the others tell him that they have seen the risen Lord. He needs to see in order to believe.

So, one week later, the disciples are gathered together again behind locked doors, and Jesus again passes through them. He invites Thomas, the Twin, to examine his body so that he can believe that Jesus has been raised from the dead. Now that Thomas has seen, he can profess that Jesus is both his Lord and his God and join the community of fellow believers. But Jesus declares blessed those who have not seen and believe. This is the Johannine author's way of bringing to an end the theme he has employed throughout his gospel: seeing a sign and believing in Jesus. If he doesn't stop this theme, then no one would be able to say he or she believes in Jesus unless he or she sees a sign that he works.

Those who have not seen yet believe are the subject of the passage from the Acts of the Apostles about the communal life embraced by the followers of Jesus. They meet together, have all things in common, and take care of each other's needs. In other words, they form an ideal community. While no community is ideal, there are many that do exist for specific purposes. For example, AA is a community of mutual support and accountability for alcoholics. Hospice is a community of men and women walking with the dying through death. A Bible study group is usually a community of people who read, study, and share their reflections on biblical texts. Just like the community formed by the first believers of Jesus for the purpose of meeting the needs of the individuals in the community, today communities are formed to meet the specific needs of the members who form the community.

Meditation
To what communities do you belong? What is the specific purpose of each?

Prayer
Your mercy endures forever, O LORD. When we were hard pressed and falling, you came to our aid with the resurrection of Jesus Christ from the dead. Help us pass through the suffering of this life to the glory of eternal life. We ask this through our Lord Jesus Christ, your Son, who lives and reigns with you and the Holy Spirit, one God, forever and ever. Amen. Alleluia!

Second Week of Easter

Second Sunday of Easter, Cycle B

Scriptures
Acts 4:32–35;
1 John 5:1–6;
John 20:19–31

Hymn
Alleluia, alleluia, alleluia!
"My wounded side, O Thomas, see;
Behold my hands, my feet," said he;
"Not faithless, but believing be." Alleluia!

"O SONS AND DAUGHTERS," VERSE 6

Reflection: The gospel passage for the Second Sunday of Easter in all three cycles is the same: John 20:19–31. It narrates the appearance of the risen Christ to his disciples on Easter Sunday evening, but Thomas is not with them. Then, a week later Jesus appears again, and this time Thomas is present. In the words of verse six of "O Sons and Daughters," Jesus tells the Twin, "My wounded side, O Thomas, see; Behold my hands, my feet. Not faithless, but believing be." And Thomas professes his faith in the resurrection by naming Jesus his Lord and his God.

Also found in all three Second Sunday of Easter cycles is the communal nature of the first followers of Jesus. In his Acts of the Apostles, the author of Luke's Gospel pictures believers being of one mind and one heart. Thinking that Jesus was returning soon, they held everything in common; thus, there were no needy people. Many sold their property and houses and gave the proceeds to the apostles, who distributed the funds according to need. This act of taking care of each other becomes a mark of the early Jesus movement. In time it gives rise to soup kitchens, hospitals, homeless shelters, and other forms of serving the common good.

Followers of Jesus of Nazareth come to understand that the love they show each other is due to the love that God has first loved each of them. In other words, God, who is love, loves people first. When people love each other, they share with each other the love that God has given to them. They know they are children of God because they love each other. Authentic love serves the other by placing him or her before one's self. In our modern world, sometimes people get so focused on God that they forget about the common good. God and the common good are not separate; they are intertwined through love.

Meditation
In what specific ways do you serve the common good?
How is each of those a reflection of God's love for you
and your response of love for the common good?

Prayer
Heavenly Father, this is the day that you have made; we are glad and rejoice in the resurrection of Jesus Christ from the grave. Grant us the Easter faith of Thomas that we may put into action the love you shower upon us. You are one God—Father, Son, and Holy Spirit—living in eternal love, now and forever and ever. Amen. Alleluia!

Second Sunday of Easter, Cycle C

Scriptures
Acts 5:12–16;
Revelation 1:9–11a, 12–13, 17–19;
John 20:19–31

Hymn
Hail him, you heirs of David's line,
Whom David Lord did call.
The God incarnate, Man divine,
And crown him Lord of all,
The God incarnate, Man divine,
And crown him Lord of all.

"ALL HAIL THE POWER OF JESUS' NAME," VERSE 3

Second Week of Easter

Reflection: Verse three of "All Hail the Power of Jesus' Name" contains two phrases worthy of deep reflection. The first is "God incarnate." The word "incarnation" comes from two Latin words meaning "in the flesh." Thus, "God incarnate" means "God in the flesh." The second phrase, "Man divine," is as oxymoronic as "God incarnate." "Man" or "human" is in opposition to the "divine" or God. Just as we do not put together God and flesh, so we do not put together man and divine. Of course, both phrases are applied to Jesus, who was God incarnate and man divine.

But today's Scripture texts also apply the man divine phrase to Peter. In the Acts of the Apostles, Peter does what Jesus did in Luke's Gospel, the first volume of a two-book work, Acts being the second volume. If Jesus healed the sick on cots and mats, Peter's shadow heals the sick and those who are mentally disturbed. Likewise, John of Patmos in the Book of Revelation is a man divine who gets caught up in spirit on the Lord's Day and sees a vision of the God incarnate. Revelation identifies the God incarnate as a son of man, who was wearing a robe with a gold sash. He identifies himself as divine, stating that he is first and last, the one who was dead and now lives. He tells John to record what he sees.

In John's Gospel, the God incarnate appears to his disciples who are huddled together behind locked doors. Their being behind locked doors indicates their disposition. However, the God incarnate opens the doors of their fear with peace, breathing the new life of the Holy Spirit into them, thus re-creating them in the same way that God once blew the breath of life into the first people he created. Thomas, who is absent on an errand, still possesses fear, but one week later Jesus blows open his locked door with peace and an invitation to see and believe in the man divine. Thomas names Jesus his Lord (man divine) and his God (incarnate).

Meditation

Using the Profession of Faith (Nicene Creed) or the Apostles' Creed underline the phrases representing God incarnate with one line and the phrases representing the man divine with two lines. What do you notice?

Prayer

Lord Jesus, you are the first and the last, the one who died and lives. You are the God incarnate and the man divine who brings our prayers to the heavenly

Father. Breathe in us the Holy Spirit that we may be re-created and come to a deeper faith in you, who live and reign with the Father and the Holy Spirit, forever and ever. Amen. Alleluia!

Monday of the Second Week of Easter

Scriptures
Acts 4:23–31;
John 3:1-8

Hymn
The Church's one foundation
Is Jesus Christ her Lord:
She is his new creation
By water and the word;
From heav'n he came and sought her
To be his holy bride;
With his own blood he bought her,
And for her life he died.

"THE CHURCH'S ONE FOUNDATION," VERSE 1

Reflection: Nicodemus is a unique character in John's Gospel who makes three separate appearances. Today's passage is the first time Nicodemus appears in the text; he comes to Jesus at night because he is literally and figuratively in the dark! Using a double entendre, the Johannine Jesus teaches him that he must be born again of water and Spirit. Nicodemus understands this to mean that he must somehow crawl back into his mother's womb and be born again, but Jesus understands this to mean baptism. To further emphasize his point, Jesus compares the elusiveness of the Spirit to wind, which blows where it wills. A person can hear it, but no one knows from where it comes or to where it goes.

Likewise, Peter, John, and others experience the Spirit shaking the place where they are gathered—what might be called a minor Pentecost. While the text does not say that an earthquake took place, it echoes the biblical manifestations of the Spirit. The Holy Spirit enables people to speak the word of God with boldness, just as it enables Jesus to speak to Nicodemus about being born again of water and the Spirit.

The first verse of "The Church's One Foundation" captures this reality. The foundation of the church is Jesus Christ, crucified and risen. The double doors into the church are word (Bible) and water (baptism) through which a person becomes a new creation. During the Easter Season, we are focused on word and water. We remember the baptisms of the Easter Vigil, when others were initiated into the church, and we remember the day of our own baptism when we were born again of water and Spirit made possible by the blood of Christ. As his bride, the church continues to swing open its doors to all who, like Nicodemus, wish to be born again.

Meditation
What do you know about your baptism? Do you know where it took place? the date? the name(s) of your godparent(s)? other circumstances?

Prayer
Sovereign LORD, maker of heaven and earth and the sea and all that is in them, once you spoke by the Holy Spirit through the mouth of your servant David. Your holy servant Jesus, whom you anointed to do your will, was crucified, but you raised him from the dead on the third day. Re-create us with the same Spirit that we may speak your word with courage and live our rebirth through water with faith. We ask this in the name of Jesus Christ, who is Lord forever and ever. Amen.

Tuesday of the Second Week of Easter

Scriptures
Acts 4:32–37;
John 3:7b–15

Hymn
Elect from ev'ry nation
Yet one o'er all the earth,

Overcome with Paschal Joy

> Her charter of salvation
> One Lord, one faith, one birth,
> One holy name she blesses,
> Partakes one holy food,
> And to one hope she presses,
> With ev'ry grace endued.
>
> "THE CHURCH'S ONE FOUNDATION," VERSE 2

Reflection: The word "one" appears seven times in verse two of "The Church's One Foundation." "One" emphasizes singularity, uniqueness, and unity. There is only one church, even though its members can be found in every nation on earth. This church is unique insofar as she has one hope fueled by grace. And this church is united through her one Lord (Jesus Christ, whose holy name she blesses), one faith, and one birth, which together form her charter of salvation. Her unity is manifested through the sharing of the bread and cup by her members.

The Scripture texts assigned to this Tuesday of the Second Week of Easter also focus on singularity, uniqueness, and unity. The community of believers in the Acts of the Apostles is of one heart and one mind. The community is unique because no one claimed any possession as his or her own; the members of the community of believers have everything in common. This commonality enhances their unity to the point that no one is needy, and those who own property or houses sell them in order to take care of the needs of others.

In the second half of the unique Johannine story about Nicodemus (the first half was read yesterday), Jesus emphasizes the singularity, uniqueness, and unity that ensue when a person is born again of water and the Spirit. Jesus tells Nicodemus that a person must be born from above. This uniqueness implies that God sends the Holy Spirit to every single person who understands Jesus' words. Out of this diversity, God creates a unity. The one who came down from heaven, Jesus, the Son of Man, is the one who goes to heaven. Like the serpent Moses erected in the desert to save the Israelites from snake bites, the Son of Man is lifted up on the cross to give new birth to those who believe in him. He gives them eternal life through rebirth in water and Spirit, forming many into one.

Second Week of Easter

Meditation
In what work of the church do you find oneness best manifested?

Prayer
Heavenly Father, from your everlasting throne you sent your Son to bear witness to heavenly things. Just as Moses lifted up the serpent in the desert, he was lifted up on the cross, but you raised him from the dead and made him the source of eternal life through the Holy Spirit. Endow us with your grace that we may be found of one heart and mind when Jesus Christ returns in glory. He is Lord forever and ever. Amen.

Wednesday of the Second Week of Easter

Scriptures
Acts 5:17–26;
John 3:16–21

Hymn
Mighty and mysterious
In the highest height,
God from everlasting,
Very Light of Light:
In the Father's bosom
With the Spirit blest,
Love, in love eternal,
Rest, in perfect rest.

"AT THE NAME OF JESUS," VERSE 3

Reflection: Verse three of "At the Name of Jesus" summarizes the passage from John's Gospel. These verses, 3:16–21, are a commentary by the narrator of the story about Nicodemus coming to Jesus at night. Jesus' words to Nicodemus end at 3:15, and the narrator begins his comments at 3:16. It is as if he is overwhelmed by the truth that he has uncovered. The mighty and mysterious God in the highest height of heaven loved the world so much that he gave his only-begotten Son from his bosom to it so that his creatures might have eternal life.

The Son, who was himself God from everlasting and light of light, was the light that came into the world, but some people preferred darkness to his light. Those who understood the truth he spoke came into his light because they saw the Son's works as done in God. In other words, they recognized God in the person of Jesus. Those who did not recognize this truth remained in darkness.

While John's Gospel does not mention the Spirit in today's passage—and because what has come to be known as Trinitarian theology was not yet developed when John's Gospel was written near the end of the first century—the third verse of "At the Name of Jesus" presents the Trinity of Father, Son, and Holy Spirit as living in eternal love and resting in perfect rest. The bond between the three persons of the Trinity is love. The Father's love eternally begets the Son, and the love of Father and Son brings about the eternal spiration of the Holy Spirit. While our language is tempered by time, eternal love indicates that the Father has always begotten the Son, and the Holy Spirit has always proceeded from the love of the Father and the Son. The three persons of the Trinity abide together in perfect rest.

Meditation

When have you been overwhelmed or overcome by God's love for you? Write a short commentary attempting to capture that experience in words.

Prayer

Father, you so loved the world you created that you gave your only-begotten Son to it so that everyone who believes in him might not perish but might have eternal life. Through his word and work, Jesus revealed the presence of the Holy Spirit, the Paraclete, and the eternal love of you, the Triune God. Hear our prayer of praise lifted to you, O Trinity, and bestow upon us eternal life now and forever and ever. Amen.

Second Week of Easter

Thursday of the Second Week of Easter

Scriptures
Acts 5:27–33;
John 3:31–36

Hymn
Through toil and tribulation
And tumult of her war
She waits the consummation
Of peace for evermore,
Till with the vision glorious
Her longing eyes are blest,
And the great Church victorious
Shall be the Church at rest.

"THE CHURCH'S ONE FOUNDATION," VERSE 3

Reflection: The trial, tribulation, and tumult mentioned in verse three of "The Church's One Foundation" is illustrated in the Acts' account of the apostles being arrested by the high priest and the Sadducees and put in the public jail, from which the angel of the Lord releases them to continue their preaching in the temple area. After a search for the prisoners, the apostles are found and brought to stand before the Sanhedrin. Peter recounts for the high priest and the members of the Sanhedrin the profession of faith: The Jewish leaders had Jesus killed by hanging him on a tree, but God raised Jesus from the dead and exalted him at his right hand as leader and savior to grant repentance to Israel and forgiveness of sins. This, of course, infuriates the leaders and makes them want to put to death the apostles.

In John's Gospel, Jesus, the one who comes from heaven, testifies to what he has seen and heard. He speaks the words of God. He shares the gift of the Holy Spirit, who enables the church to wait patiently for the consummation of eternal peace. The Johannine Jesus instills a glorious vision of life eternal in those who follow him. It is his vision of rest from trial, tribulation, and tumult that keeps the longing alive.

Overcome with Paschal Joy

No one is immune from trial, tribulation, and tumult. While we may not be arrested by religious leaders and put in prison, we may find our hope under attack by the popular culture in which we live. For example, the dignity of human life is attacked from conception to its natural end. Moral behavior is criticized as being caught in the Dark Ages and in desperate need of reform. Justice is tempered by consumerism, jurisprudence by revenge, and health by smoking, over-eating, and illegal drug use. Those are some of the trials, tribulations, and tumults that the church in the modern world faces today.

Meditation
How do you face modern trials, tribulations, and tumults
and keep the glorious vision of the church alive?

Prayer
All holy God, you are close to the brokenhearted, and you save those who are crushed in spirit. When we face modern trials, tribulations, and tumults, keep us faithful to our faith and your church. We ask this through our Lord Jesus Christ, your Son, who lives and reigns with you and the Holy Spirit, one God, forever and ever. Amen.

Friday of the Second Week of Easter

Scriptures
Acts 5:34–42;
John 6:1–15

Hymn
All hail the pow'r of Jesus' name!
Let angels prostrate fall;
Bring forth the royal diadem,
And crown him Lord of all,
Bring forth the royal diadem,
And crown him Lord of all.

"ALL HAIL THE POWER OF JESUS' NAME," VERSE 1

Second Week of Easter

Reflection: Just as Jesus' name is the subject of the first verse of "All hail the Power of Jesus' Name," so it is the subject of the Scripture texts assigned for this Friday of the Second Week of Easter. Repeatedly, the apostles have been ordered by the high priest and the members of the Sanhedrin to stop speaking of and in the name of Jesus. Of course, they do not stop, and they are arrested repeatedly and put in prison. Once they are released they rejoice that they have been found worthy to suffer dishonor for the sake of the name Jesus.

The passage from John's Gospel begins an eight-weekday-long process of reading all of chapter six of the Fourth Gospel. Commonly known as the bread of life discourse, it begins with Jesus going up a mountain, seeing a large crowd of people coming to him, and feeding them with five barley loaves and two fish. Once the people witness this sign, they hail the power of his name by identifying him as the prophet—that is, the prophet like Moses—who was to come into the world. In order to keep them from declaring him to be their king and crowning him with a royal diadem, Jesus disappears on the mountain alone.

While the verse of the hymn sings about angels falling prostrate at Jesus' name, the liturgy of the Roman Catholic Church directs that all make a profound bow when reciting "and by the Holy Spirit was incarnate of the Virgin Mary, and became man" in the Nicene Creed. Also, a bow of the head is made when the three Divine Persons are named together and at the name of Jesus, the Blessed Virgin Mary, and the saint of the day. A bow signifies reverence and honor shown to those receiving the bow or to signs that represent them, such as the altar and the body and blood of Christ under the forms of bread and wine.

Meditation

Do you find yourself bowing during the liturgy?
Do you find yourself bowing during times of personal prayer?
What does the bow represent to you?

Prayer

You, LORD, are our light and our salvation; we have nothing to fear. We seek to dwell in your house all the days of our life that we may gaze upon your loveliness, contemplate your dwelling place, and bow before you. Grant us a deeper respect for your name, Father, for that of your Son, Jesus Christ, and for that of the Holy Spirit. You dwell in perfect Trinity forever and ever. Amen.

Saturday of the Second Week of Easter

Scriptures
Acts 6:1–7;
John 6:16–21

Hymn
The King of love my shepherd is,
Whose goodness fails me never;
I nothing lack if I am his,
And he is mine for ever.

"THE KING OF LOVE MY SHEPHERD IS," VERSE 1

Reflection: The first verse of "The King of Love My Shepherd Is" aptly summarizes the Scripture texts given for this last day of the Second Week of Easter. Jesus is portrayed as the shepherd whose goodness watches over the church, the boat tossed by the stirred sea and the strong winds of the world. After he had multiplied the five barley loaves and two fish, Jesus disappeared on the mountain to be alone. While his disciples are being tossed by the sea and the wind, he comes walking on the water toward them. He does not fail them.

Following the pattern the author of Luke's Gospel and the Acts of the Apostles has established, the apostles in the Acts do what Jesus did in the gospel. In today's passage they appoint seven men to take care of the daily distribution of food to the widows. In Luke's Gospel, Jesus appoints twelve and seventy(-two) to preach the word of God. In the Acts, the apostles appoint seven to show that those who are hungry will lack nothing if they belong to followers of Jesus of Nazareth.

It is important to note that in the Acts passage the apostles do not choose the seven men to wait on tables. They call together the community and ask the members to select from among themselves seven reputable men, who are filled with the Holy Spirit and wisdom. Once the community

Second Week of Easter

names Stephen, Philip, Prochorus, Nicanor, Timon, Parmenas, and Nicholas, they are presented to the apostles who pray and lay hands on their heads, giving them the shepherding authority to meet the needs of widows, both Hellenists and Hebrews.

Meditation
In the church today, where do you find the practice
of nominating people for ministry
and having leaders pray for them
and lay their hands upon them,
giving them the authority to shepherd a part of Christ's flock?

Prayer
Lord Jesus Christ, King of love, you shepherd your church through all the strong winds of time. Help us to trust your guidance and to know your never-failing goodness. Lacking nothing, we are yours, and you are ours forever and ever. Amen.

10

Third Week of Easter

Third Sunday of Easter, Cycle A

Scriptures
Acts 2:14, 22–33;
1 Peter 1:17–21;
Luke 24:13–35

Hymn
You chosen seed of Israel's race,
A remnant weak and small,
Hail him who saved you by his grace,
And crown him Lord of all,
Hail him who saved you by his grace,
And crown him Lord of all.

"ALL HAIL THE POWER OF JESUS' NAME," VERSE 4

Reflection: It is very easy for modern people to forget that the movement known as Christianity began among a remnant of Jews who were themselves a minority within a minority. Once the Jews had returned to Jerusalem from Babylonian captivity, they enjoyed a period of self-rule which lasted but a few years before the Roman Empire conquered the known world and them. Jesus grew up among and spoke to the chosen seed of Israel's race, a remnant weak and small, about the kingdom of God. Out of those people, a minority, came his followers, a minority within a minority.

It is to those people that Peter's Pentecost speech is addressed; a portion of that speech forms today's first reading. Peter names his listeners as Jews as well as their previous name of Israelites. He declares that what happened to Jesus of Nazareth—death and resurrection—was according to the set plan and foreknowledge of God, who commended his Son to them with mighty deeds, wonders, and signs. Now that he has been exalted at God's right hand, he has poured the Holy Spirit on those who believe in him.

The First Letter of St. Peter echoes verse four of "All Hail the Power of Jesus' Name" when it states that the readers have been ransomed from their previous way of life with the precious blood of Christ, a spotless unblemished lamb. They have been saved by Christ's grace. Therefore, the One who was known before the foundation of the world, but revealed in their own time, has been raised from the dead by God and given glory. They have been given faith and hope that enable them to crown Jesus as Lord of all.

Meditation
What small event in your life led to something big with Christ's grace?

Prayer
O LORD, our hearts are glad and our souls rejoice because you did not abandon your Son to the netherworld, nor did you allow your faithful One to undergo corruption. You showed him the path to life, raised him from the dead to abounding joy in your presence, and crowned him Lord of all. Grant that we, your chosen ones, though weak and small, may be saved by his grace and share his life forever. We ask this through the same Jesus Christ, our Lord, who lives and reigns with you and the Holy Spirit, one God, forever and ever. Amen.

Third Sunday of Easter, Cycle B

Scriptures
Acts 3:13–15, 17–19;
1 John 2:1–5a;
Luke 24:35–38

Overcome with Paschal Joy

Hymn

Where the paschal blood is poured,
Death's dread angel sheathes his sword;
Israel's hosts triumphant go,
Through the wave that drowns the foe.
Christ the Lamb, whose blood was shed,
Paschal victim, paschal bread!
With sincerity and love
Eat we manna from above.

"AT THE LAMB'S HIGH FEAST WE SING," VERSE 2

Reflection: The word "paschal" occurs three times in verse two of "At the Lamb's High Feast We Sing." Paschal describes both Jewish Passover and Christian Easter. The reference to paschal blood comes from the Exodus story of the Hebrews taking the blood of a lamb and smearing it on the doorposts and lintels of their homes. The angel of death sees the blood and sheathes his sword near Hebrew homes, but kills the firstborn of people and animals in Egypt. That Passover permits the next to take place. Moses leads the Hebrews to the Sea of Reeds, which he parts so Israel's hosts can pass through it. The people pass over triumphantly; however, Pharaoh's army is drowned by the wave of water that engulfs it, as the water flows back to its place.

The rest of verse two of "At the Lamb's High Feast We Sing" is about Christian Easter, whose meaning derives from Jewish Passover. Jesus is named as the new paschal lamb, whose blood was shed on the cross to wipe away people's sins, to be expiation for the sins of the whole world. Like the Passover lamb of old, Jesus is a paschal victim; he is also paschal bread. As a paschal victim, he died on the cross. As paschal bread, he is known to his followers when they gather to break bread in his memory. Those who eat this paschal bread with sincerity and love eat manna from above, just like the Israelites did in the desert.

The Scripture texts for this Third Sunday of Easter further emphasize the paschal character of this fifty-day season. In the Acts of the Apostles, Peter reminds his hearers that the author of life, Jesus, was put to death, but God raised him from the dead. In other words, he passed over from death to life. The First Letter of John calls him Jesus Christ the righteous one, the Advocate with the Father. And Luke's Gospel narrates a post-paschal appearance during which he teaches them that it was written that he would suffer and rise from the dead on the third day. Using the second verse from "At the Lamb's High Feast We Sing," it is easy to see how the paschal lamb in the Hebrew Bible (Old Testament) prepared for the paschal lamb, Jesus, in the Christian Bible (New Testament).

Meditation
What associations does the word "paschal" have for you?

Prayer
Creator God, once you saved your people with the blood of the paschal lamb and led them through the sea that drowned their foes. You made your Son a paschal lamb and saved all people with his blood shed on the cross. As we eat his paschal bread and drink his paschal blood, grant that we may pass over from death to eternal life. He lives and reigns with you and the Holy Spirit, one God, forever and ever. Amen.

Third Sunday of Easter, Cycle C

Scriptures
Acts 5:27–32, 40b–41;
Revelation 5:11–14;
John 21:1–19

Hymn
As sinners let us not forget,
The wormwood and the gall;
We spread our trophies at his feet,
And crown him Lord of all,
We spread our trophies at his feet,
And crown him Lord of all.

"ALL HAIL THE POWER OF JESUS' NAME," VERSE 5

Overcome with Paschal Joy

Reflection: Everyone loves getting a trophy, a token of victory. It may be a cup, a shield, a plaque, a medal, or a statue given as an award in acknowledgement of a victory, success, or some other achievement in sports, academics, or careers. Everyone has seen the victor lift into the air the trophy so that all can see it and, then, bring it to his or her lips and kiss it while photographers snap hundreds of pictures. Trophies, displayed on mantels, bookcases, and shelves in homes, make those who have won them feel important.

Verse five of "All Hail the Power of Jesus' Name" diminishes the value of our human trophies. It states that we spread our trophies at Jesus' feet because he won a far greater victory over sin and death. Today's passage from the Book of Revelation presents Jesus as such a victor, a slain lamb, who receives power, riches, wisdom, strength, honor, glory, and blessing. Even the twenty-four elders fall down and worship him. In other words, they spread their trophies at his feet.

In the passage from the added chapter to John's Gospel, Jesus demonstrates his victory over death by appearing to seven of his disciples while they are fishing and catching nothing. He instructs them where to drop the net, and they drag in a net full of fish. Then, he prepares breakfast for them, breaking bread, and disclosing his victorious presence. He concludes by requesting that Simon Peter crown him Lord of all by three-times feeding his lambs and sheep as demonstration of his love. This not only rehabilitates Simon Peter's three-fold denial earlier in the gospel, but it gives him the opportunity to follow Jesus again.

Meditation
What trophy do you need to place at Jesus' feet?

Prayer
Worthy are you, Lamb of God that was slain, to receive power and riches, wisdom and strength, honor and glory and blessing from all whom you have rescued from sin and death. Hear our praise, Lord Jesus Christ, as we join the heavenly chorus giving you blessing and honor, glory and might, forever and ever. Amen.

Third Week of Easter

Monday of the Third Week of Easter

Scriptures
Acts 6:8–15;
John 6:22–29

Hymn
Mighty victim from the sky,
Pow'rs of hell beneath you lie;
Death is conquered in the fight,
You have brought us life and light.
Your victorious banner wave;
You have risen from the grave.
You have opened paradise,
And in you all saints shall rise.

"AT THE LAMB'S HIGH FEAST WE SING," VERSE 3

Reflection: Today's passage from the Acts of the Apostles is the first part of a two-day story about St. Stephen, the first Christian martyr for whom Christ opened paradise; the name "Stephen" means "crown." Stephen, one of those seven men previously chosen to wait on tables, is filled with grace and power. Those with whom he debates cannot withstand the wisdom and the Spirit with which he speaks. So, they incite others to accuse him falsely of speaking against the basic tenets of Judaism. However, Stephen has been speaking about Jesus of Nazareth.

The Johannine Jesus of Nazareth begins his reflection on the multiplication of five barley loaves and two fish in the gospel. The people who have sought him hear him declare that they should be working for food that endures for eternal life by believing in him and not merely be satisfied with earthly food. In the words of verse three of "At the Lamb's High Feast We Sing," Jesus is the mighty victim from the sky who has conquered death and brought life and light to people. Upon him God has set his seal. Those who believe in him and eat his body and drink his blood have eternal life.

As we continue our celebration of this Easter Season waving the banner of Jesus' resurrection, we do well to reflect upon the multiplication of loaves and fish. Like those in the gospel account, we are drawn to this wonderful deed, but Jesus points us beyond the deed to its meaning or sign value. According to the Johannine author, the sign points toward another reality, namely, that God has offered eternal life to people through faith in Jesus. Just like bread and fish keep us alive physically, the body and blood of the risen Christ keep us alive eternally. This is what Stephen knew and for which he received the crown of eternal life.

Meditation
What are your personal reflections
on the multiplication of barley loaves and fish?
What strength do you receive from your meditation?

Prayer
God of Stephen, you filled your martyr with grace and power and gave him wisdom and Spirit so that he might speak to your people about your Son, our Lord Jesus Christ. Place on our lips your words that we might proclaim to all we meet the One upon whom you placed your seal, the same Jesus Christ, risen from the dead and Lord forever and ever. Amen.

Tuesday of the Third Week of Easter

Scriptures
Acts 7:51–8:1a;
John 6:30–35

Hymn
Crown him, you martyrs of our God,
Who from his altar call;
Praise him whose way of pain your trod,
And crown him Lord of all,
Praise him whose way of pain you trod,
And crown him Lord of all.

"ALL HAIL THE POWER OF JESUS' NAME," VERSE 2

Third Week of Easter

Reflection: As the author of Luke's Gospel and the Acts of the Apostles loves to do, he presents St. Stephen as Jesus. Stephen's Feast as the first Christian martyr occurs on the day after Christmas. However, remembering his death and resurrection is appropriate during the Easter Season because he crowned (the name "Stephen" means "crown") Christ as Lord of all through the way of pain he trod. Today's passage from the Acts of the Apostles presents Stephen as following in the footsteps of the martyrdom of Jesus in Luke's Gospel. Like Jesus, Stephen, filled with the Holy Spirit, sees heaven opened and the glory of God and Jesus at God's right hand. Like Jesus entrusted his spirit to God, Stephen commends his spirit to the Lord Jesus. And like Jesus forgave those who crucified him, Stephen asks God not to hold the sin of his death against those who are stoning him to death.

The passage from John's Gospel continues Jesus' reflections on the multiplication of the barley loaves and fish. He moves the meditation forward by reminding his hearers that the Israelites once ate manna in the desert. The manna was heavenly bread given by God to satisfy the hunger of his chosen people. Jesus, however, declares that he is the bread from heaven that now gives life to the world. Whoever eats of him, that is, whoever believes in him, will never hunger or thirst.

It is Jesus as bread that strengthened Stephen to face his martyrdom. While only a part of his long speech is given in today's passage, the reader would do well to read Acts 7:1–60. It presents a summary of God's work in the Hebrew Bible (Old Testament) and the inability of his chosen people often to understand it. Maybe from the example of Stephen we can learn the lesson that others have failed to comprehend.

Meditation

What work of God in your life do you not understand?
How can Stephen's speech shed light upon your lack of understanding?

Prayer

Ever-living God, your martyr Stephen crowned your Son Lord of all through his suffering and death. Grant us the grace to follow in the footsteps of Stephen, who calls us from your altar to profess faith in Jesus Christ, who lives and reigns with you and the Holy Spirit, one God, forever and ever. Amen.

Overcome with Paschal Joy

Wednesday of the Third Week of Easter

Scriptures
Acts 8:1b–8;
John 6:35–40

Hymn
There we shall with you remain, Alleluia!
Partners of your endless reign; Alleluia!
We shall see you face to face, Alleluia!
You, our hearts' true resting place. Alleluia!

"HAIL THE DAY THAT SEES HIM RISE," VERSE 6

Reflection: The sixth verse of "Hail the Day That Sees Him Rise" is addressed to the risen and ascended Christ, who has prepared a place for us in the heavens. As his partners, we share in his kingdom; we see him face to face; and we find rest from our labors on earth. This verse summarizes the hope that is found in both of the Scripture texts assigned to this Wednesday of the Third Week of Easter.

As a result of the death of Stephen, a persecution breaks out; this causes many of the believers to scatter around the country outside Jerusalem. Saul, otherwise known as Paul, who had been present at Stephen's stoning, seeks men and women who follow Jesus of Nazareth; he drags them from their homes and imprisons them. However, in the midst of this persecution, hope arises. Philip, another one of those seven men chosen to wait on tables with Stephen, has success in preaching in Samaria. Like Jesus, he worked signs, cast out unclean spirits, and healed many paralyzed and crippled people. These deeds not only give hope to those who see the signs and are cured, but it also gives hope to those suffering persecution.

Hope is also present in the gospel passage which continues the Johannine Jesus' bread of life discourse. He makes it clear that his Father's will is that everyone who sees the Son and believes in him may have eternal life, and he will raise believers on the last day. His mission from his Father is to do his Father's will and not to lose anyone the Father has given to him. That is a great hope based on Jesus being the bread of life to satisfy all hunger.

Third Week of Easter

Meditation
What is your greatest hope?

Prayer
Father, we sing joyfully to you and praise the glory of your name. Through the death and resurrection of your Son, you have filled us with new hope of life beyond the grave. There, we hope to see you face to face in the endless reign of Jesus Christ and find the true resting place in the Holy Spirit. You are one God, forever and ever. Amen.

Thursday of the Third Week of Easter

Scriptures
Acts 8:26–40;
John 6:44–51

Hymn
Alleluia! Bread of angels,
And on earth our food, our stay;
Alleluia! Here the sinful
Flee to you from day to day;
Intercessor, friend of sinners,
Earth's Redeemer, plead for me,
Where the songs of all the sinless
Sweep across the crystal sea.

"ALLELUIA! SING TO JESUS," VERSE 3

Reflection: Verse three from "Alleluia! Sing to Jesus" summarizes both Scripture passages assigned for this Thursday of the Third Week of Easter. In John's Gospel, Jesus continues his bread of life discourse about being the bread of life, that is, the living bread that came down from heaven. In the words of verse three, he is the bread of angels. On earth he is our food to eat and to live forever. The Israelites ate manna in the desert, but they died. Those who eat the bread of angels will not die.

In the Acts passage, Philip, one of the seven men chosen by the community and delegated by the apostles to wait on tables, sets out on a journey through the desert where he meets an Ethiopian eunuch, who is reading the scroll of the prophet Isaiah about the suffering servant of the LORD. Philip identifies Jesus as the one who was like a sheep led to the slaughter. In response to Philip's proclamation, the sinful Ethiopian requests baptism. He has come to faith in the intercessor, Jesus Christ, who is the friend of sinners and earth's redeemer. Philip baptizes him in some water along the way, disappears, and continues to proclaim the good news elsewhere. We presume that the redeemed Ethiopian continued on his way.

The offer of eternal life that Jesus presents in John's Gospel and the offer of salvation that the Ethiopian eunuch possesses while reading the prophet Isaiah are offered to us. That's why the last few words of verse three of "Alleluia! Sing to Jesus" end with the request addressed to Jesus to plead for us. Our desire, after accepting the offer, is one day to join in the endless song in the kingdom, where the chaos of the sea has been turned to crystal calm.

Meditation

What has God offered to you and you accepted?
What difference has that made in your life?

Prayer

Almighty Father, you offer life to all people through the death and resurrection of your Son, Jesus Christ. After hearing his words, give us the grace to respond to your offer that we, who have eaten the bread of life, may be brought to eternal life. We ask this through the same Jesus Christ, who is Lord forever and ever. Amen.

Friday of the Third Week of Easter

Scriptures

Acts 9:1–20;
John 6:52–59

Third Week of Easter

Hymn

King of kings, yet born of Mary, as of old on earth he stood,
Lord of lords in human vesture; in the Body and the Blood
He will give to all the faithful his own self for heav'nly food.

"LET ALL MORTAL FLESH KEEP SILENCE," VERSE 2

Reflection: In the passage from the Acts of the Apostles, we are presented the Saul (Paul) of the Acts; Saul (Paul) is Luke's idealized apostle to the Gentiles who first appears at the stoning of Stephen. Luke's Saul (Paul) is a destroyer of those who follow the Way, what would later be known as Christianity. However, God has other plans for him, and he begins to enact those plans with a blinding light and a disciple named Ananias. Once Saul's (Paul's) conversion is complete, he begins to proclaim that the King of kings, born of Mary, who once stood on the earth in human vesture, is the Son of God.

Today's passage from John's Gospel continues the bread of life discourse. Here, too, God has a plan different from the Jews, who want to know how Jesus can give his flesh to eat and his blood to drink. To them this sounds like cannibalism. God's plan, however, is to give his people the body and blood of his Son under the forms of bread and wine. Just as usual bread and wine give life to those who eat and drink, so those who eat and drink of the body and blood of the Lord of lords receive heavenly food for eternal life.

In our modern world, God's plan is seldom our plan! Because we live in a culture that fosters individuality and personal mission or career—which in themselves are not bad—God's plan often takes second place to our plans. A college student may say that his plan is to be a computer informationist technologist, but God may have another plan for him. A young woman may have the plan to be a nurse, but God may have another plan for her. Countless young men and women pursue careers in various fields, but one day they wake up and realize that is not God's plan for them. So, like Saul (Paul) and the Jews at the time of Jesus, adjustments need to be made so that they are living their lives according to God's plan.

Overcome with Paschal Joy

Meditation
As you look back through the years of your life,
what have you come to understand to be God's plan for you?

Prayer
Heavenly Father, your ways are not our ways, and so we struggle to know your will that we may do it. Your Son, the King of kings and Lord of lords, taught this truth both to his own people and to Saul (Paul). Help us to learn this great truth as we feast on the heavenly food of the body and blood of Jesus Christ, who lives and reigns with you and the Holy Spirit, one God, forever and ever. Amen.

Saturday of the Third Week of Easter

Scriptures
Acts 9:31–42;
John 6:60–69

Hymn
Let all mortal flesh keep silence, and with fear and trembling stand;
Ponder nothing earthy minded, for with blessing in his hand
Christ our God to earth descendeth, our full homage to demand.

"LET ALL MORTAL FLESH KEEP SILENCE," VERSE 1

Reflection: The first verse of "Let All Mortal Flesh Keep Silence" urges us, mortal flesh, to keep silence and to stand with fear and trembling before the mystery of Christ descending to earth. The end of the discourse on the bread of life from John's Gospel presumes that Jesus has descended from heaven to earth with blessing in his hand for those who believe in him. In today's passage he asks those who are finding his teaching hard to ingest if they would be even more shocked if they saw him ascending to where he was before.

While it may not at first be obvious that there is a descent in the passage from the Acts of the Apostles, upon closer examination we find it. In

Luke's two volume work, the Gospel According to Luke and the Acts of the Apostles, whatever Jesus does in volume one, Peter (and Paul) does (do) in volume two. In other words, Peter (and Paul) is a new Jesus. So, if Jesus healed a paralyzed man in Luke's Gospel, Peter heals Aeneas in the Acts. If Jesus raises someone from the dead in Luke's Gospel, Peter raises Tabitha from the dead in the Acts. Thus, Jesus descends into Peter in order for him to accomplish such mighty deeds.

Christ our God continues to descend to earth in many different ways. For example, he descends in those who volunteer to serve in a soup kitchen, distribute back-to-school supplies in shelters, and build houses for Habitat for Humanity. You may see him in the minister who has pondered the Scripture texts for a given Sunday and exposes the depth of the inspired meaning. Christ descends in the stranger we greet on the sidewalk, the person who lets us get into the flow of traffic on a busy street, the clerk who smiles at us in the grocery store or in the department store. Our only response is to enjoy a moment of silent fear and trembling while pondering the divine blessing descending upon us and to give Christ our full homage.

Meditation

What has been your most recent experience
of Christ our God descending to earth?

Prayer

Mighty God, when we recognize your presence in your Son descending to the earth, all we can do is pay him homage with holy silence. Give all of us clothed in mortal flesh the blessings that you promise to those who follow your Son, Jesus Christ, who lives and reigns with you and the Holy Spirit, one God, forever and ever. Amen.

11

Fourth Week of Easter

Fourth Sunday of Easter, Cycle A

Scriptures
Acts 2:14a, 36–41;
Peter 2:20b–25;
John 10:1–10

Hymn
To God and to the Lamb, I will sing, I will sing;
To God and to the Lamb I will sing.
To God and to the Lamb Who is the great I am,
While millions join the theme, I will sing, I will sing;
While millions join the theme, I will sing.

"WHAT WONDROUS LOVE IS THIS?" VERSE 2

Reflection: In John's Gospel and in the Book of Revelation, Jesus is hailed as the Lamb of God. That is why the second verse of "What Wondrous Love Is This?" presents the first-person singer declaring that he or she will sing to God and the Lamb, who is the great I AM. The great I AM is, of course, God. In the Book of Exodus when Moses asks God for his name, the LORD tells him that he is I AM. Thus, while millions of people join the song, praise is sung to God and the Lamb.

Fourth Week of Easter

This Fourth Sunday of Easter is commonly known as good shepherd Sunday because of the passage from John's Gospel that is read. While Jesus doesn't identify himself as the good shepherd in today's passage, he does declare, ". . . I am the gate for the sheep" (John 10:7). He, God, is the portal through whom the sheep pass to God and salvation. Jesus is the shepherd of the sheep for whom the gatekeeper opens the door into the sheepfold. The sheep know him and follow him.

While modern people get all caught up in the emotion of Psalm 23:1—"The LORD is my shepherd"—being referred to as sheep was an insult in the ancient world. Sheep are very dumb animals; that is why they need to the constant supervision of a shepherd, a dog, or a llama. Even the passage from the First Letter of Peter notes that people had gone astray like sheep, but have now returned to the shepherd and guardian of their souls. In the gospel, the Pharisees fail to understand what Jesus is teaching because they considered themselves the shepherd of the sheep. However, he reduces them to the status of sheep, who do not listen to the shepherd. Jesus, the shepherd, has come that the sheep may have abundant life.

Meditation
In what specific ways is Jesus your shepherd?
Do you enter the church through him,
recognizing his voice in the Scriptures and following him?

Prayer
To you, Almighty God, and to your Son, the Lamb, and to the Holy Spirit, we sing. You are the great I AM who calls his people to follow him. Through the ministry of Jesus, your servant, you established a new sheepfold with your Son as the gate. Keep far from us the thieves and robbers who try to steal us from him, who is Lord forever and ever. Amen.

Overcome with Paschal Joy

Fourth Sunday of Easter, Cycle B

Scriptures

Acts 4:8–12;
1 John 3:1–2;
John 10:11–18

Hymn

At the name of Jesus
Ev'ry knee shall bow,
Ev'ry tongue confess him
King of glory now.
'Tis the Father's pleasure
We should call him Lord
Who from the beginning
Was the mighty Word.

"AT THE NAME OF JESUS," VERSE 1

Reflection: The first verse of "At the Name of Jesus" captures the essence of the Scripture texts for this Fourth Sunday of Easter. In the passage from John's Gospel, the presupposition gained from the first chapter of John is that Jesus is God's mighty Word from the beginning. This is developed throughout John's Gospel and continues to be exposed in the mighty words he speaks about being the good shepherd who lays down his life for his sheep. On this good shepherd Sunday, the Johannine Jesus makes very clear that he is, oxymoronically, the good shepherd. In Jesus' time, there was no such thing as a good shepherd; all shepherds were bad because they lived in the fields and smelled like sheep! Unlike other shepherds, who see the wolf coming and run away, Jesus lays down his life for his sheep. Furthermore, he knows his sheep, and they know him by name and voice.

In the passage from the Acts of the Apostles—a part of a longer speech given after Peter and John have healed a crippled man—Peter reminds his listeners that the crippled man was healed in the name of Jesus Christ the

Nazarene, who was crucified and raised by God from the dead. Peter also states that there is no other name under heaven given to humankind by which it is to be saved.

Therefore, at the name of Jesus every knee should bend in a genuflection, and every tongue should confess that Jesus, once crucified, has been raised from the dead and is the king of glory. Once God raised him from the dead, the Father took pleasure in us calling him Lord, that is, Master. He has made us children of God now. However, his resurrection gives us hope that there is more to come, but that more to come has not yet been revealed. We do know that when it is revealed that we shall be like the king of glory and see him as he is in glory at the Father's right side.

Meditation
What is your favorite name for Jesus: Christ, good shepherd, word, etc.?
What are the implications of that name for you?

Prayer
Heavenly Father, at the name of Jesus every knee bends on earth and every tongue confesses him to be king of glory, for by raising him from the dead, you established him as Lord of earth and heaven. Keep us faithful in following the good shepherd who laid down his life for his sheep. He is Lord forever and ever. Amen.

Fourth Sunday of Easter, Cycle C

Scriptures
Acts 13:14, 43–52;
Revelation 7:9, 14b–17;
John 10:27–30

Hymn
Let ev'ry tribe and ev'ry tongue
Respond to Jesus' call,
Lift high the universal song
And crown him Lord of all,

Overcome with Paschal Joy

> Lift high the universal song,
> And crown him Lord of all.

"ALL HAIL THE POWER OF JESUS' NAME," VERSE 6

Reflection: The vision of the great multitude that John of Patmos records in the Book of Revelation with people from every nation, race, people, and tongue is put into song with verse six of "All Hail the Power of Jesus' Name." Those of every tribe and every tongue have survived the time of great distress. They are the sheep who have heard the call of the shepherd; Jesus gives them eternal life as they sing the universal song that crowns him Lord of all.

As narrated in the passage from the Acts of the Apostles, Paul and Barnabas bring the good news of God, namely, the story of the death and resurrection of Jesus, to the Jews first, and a few listen and believe the word of the Lord. However, many, according to the Acts, reject the words of Paul and Barnabas. So, the two shake the dust from their feet, an ancient sign of protest, and make the object of their mission the Gentiles. This is a dramatic turn in the ministry of Paul and Barnabas. Biblically, the whole world is divided between Jews and Gentiles. When the Jews reject the good news, the Gentiles are delighted that they can hear it, and the word of the Lord continues to spread through the ministry of Paul and Barnabas.

Before Paul and Barnabas the Christian perspective was very narrow. Since Jesus was a Jew, who preached to his fellow Jews and called some of them to be his apostles, the first to hear about his death and resurrection were the Jews. But the perspective expanded to the Gentiles with Paul and Barnabas. They realized that it was not just the chosen people who were called; through Jesus, God has called all people—every tribe and every tongue—to respond to his crucified, dead, and risen Son. Paul and Barnabas lifted high the universal song that has continued to echo throughout the world for two thousand years. While at time some people want to narrow the perspective, the ministry of Paul and Barnabas continues to widen it.

Fourth Week of Easter

Meditation
How broad is your Christian perspective?
Think about what may narrow it by excluding groups from it
and how you can keep that from happening.

Prayer
Lord Jesus, you are the Lamb at the center of the throne shepherding people of every nation, race, people, and tongue. Today we come before you with joyful song, responding to your call, and singing the universal song. You are Lord of all forever and ever. Amen.

Monday of the Fourth Week of Easter

Scriptures
Acts 11:1–18;
John 10:1–10 (Year A) or
John 10:11–18 (Years B and C)

Hymn
Shepherd of souls, refresh and bless
Your chosen pilgrim flock
With manna in the wilderness
With water from the rock.

"SHEPHERD OF SOULS," VERSE 1

Reflection: No matter what the Sunday cycle, today's gospel passage from John continues either Jesus as the good shepherd reflection or Jesus as the gate for the sheep which was begun yesterday. The shepherd of souls who is asked to refresh and bless the pilgrim flock in verse one of "Shepherd of Souls" is God. And that is exactly what God does in the passage from the Acts of the Apostles. First, however, we need to establish a basic presumption of the account of Peter's entering a Gentile's home and eating with him and his family.

Overcome with Paschal Joy

Peter, a circumcised Jew, should not have entered a Gentile family's home nor should he have dined there. Gentiles are uncircumcised; thus, they are unclean. They are so unclean, that we frequently find them being called dogs by Jews in the Bible. So, the apostles and other believers in Jerusalem—the circumcised Jews—hear that the Gentiles have accepted the word of God, but Peter has violated the law by entering their home and eating with them. Peter narrates a visionary experience he had of a sheet coming down from the heavens filled with clean and unclean animals. Peter is told to eat, but he objects that he cannot eat unclean animal flesh. God tells him that what the Holy One has declared to be clean Peter must not name as profane.

For Peter and for Jewish believers in Jerusalem this vision is enough to convince them that the trance has a direct application to Peter's actions. After Peter spoke to the Gentiles, they received the Holy Spirit, and then they were baptized. This leads all to declare that God has granted life-giving repentance to the Gentiles. And that is quite a statement for a Jew to make! Receiving the Holy Spirit is like eating manna in the wilderness; it is like drinking the water flowing from the rock in the desert. The Gentiles have received the same gift of salvation that God offered to the Jews through faith in the Lord Jesus Christ. God has created one pilgrim flock from two different groups of sheep.

Meditation
Today, where do you see God doing extraordinary things like he did through Peter?

Prayer
Shepherd of souls, you gave your chosen people manna in the wilderness and water to drink from the rock. Through your Son, you gave life-giving repentance to the Gentiles. Refresh and bless us, your chosen pilgrim flock, with the gift of the Holy Spirit that we may discern your will and do it. We ask this through our Lord Jesus Christ, your Son, who lives and reigns with you and the Holy Spirit, one God, forever and ever. Amen.

Fourth Week of Easter

Tuesday of the Fourth Week of Easter

Scriptures
Acts 11:19–26;
John 10:22–30

Hymn
The King of love my shepherd is,
Whose goodness fails me never;
I nothing lack if I am his,
And he is mine for ever.

"THE KING OF LOVE MY SHEPHERD IS," VERSE 1

Reflection: The setting for the passage from John's Gospel is the Feast of the Dedication of the Temple, better known as Hanukkah. It is important to pay attention to this important note in John's Gospel, because the Johannine Jesus replaces all temple feasts with himself. The king of love addresses those Jews marking this winter celebration. He tells them that they are not among his sheep because they do not hear his voice and follow him. Those who do hear him and follow him receive eternal life. In the words of verse one of "The King of Love My Shepherd Is," his goodness never fails them. Furthermore, they lack nothing because the Father has given them to Jesus, and no one can take them out of the Father's hand.

After the Acts of the Apostles portrays Peter launching the mission to the Gentiles following his vision, the author removes Peter from the story and turns to focus on Barnabas and Saul (Paul) and their missions to the Gentiles. Thus, from the middle of the eleventh chapter of Acts the Jewish mission is a past event; what lies ahead to the end of the book are the exploits of Saul (Paul) to carry God's word to the Gentiles. Greek-speaking people (Gentiles) hear the Lord Jesus proclaimed; because the hand of the Lord is with them, a great number who believe turn to the Lord. As the numbers increase, Barnabas is sent to Antioch to investigate. He discovers the grace of God everywhere. Barnabas himself is a man filled with the Holy Spirit and faith.

However, he needs help in this mission to the Gentiles. So, he goes off to Tarsus to look for Saul (Paul) and brings him back to Antioch. Together they teach a large number of Gentiles. According to the author of the Acts of the Apostles, it is in Antioch that disciples are first called Christians, that is, followers of Jesus Christ. We don't want to think that the mission to the Gentiles was a thing of the past. It continues today through the example that Christian neighbors set. It can be found when people stand up for social justice, fair wages for a fair day's work, and the right to life from conception to natural death. While some people think that door-to-door evangelization is the only way to be a missionary, there are many other ways to bring the good news to people.

Meditation
What are the methods of your missionary work?

Prayer
Almighty God, you are the king of love and shepherd of our souls whose goodness never fails us. After your Son, Jesus Christ, suffered death, he lacked nothing because you raised him to new life. Give us the Holy Spirit that we lack nothing in your service. We ask this in the name of the same Christ our Lord. Amen.

Wednesday of the Fourth Week of Easter

Scriptures
Acts 12:24–13:5a;
John 12:44–50

Hymn
Bore it up triumphant
With its human light,
Through all ranks of creatures
To the central height,
To the throne of Godhead,
To the Father's breast;

Fourth Week of Easter

Filled it with the glory
Of that perfect rest.

"AT THE NAME OF JESUS," VERSE 5

Reflection: The "it" in the second word of verse five of "At the Name of Jesus" is "the name Jesus." Basically, this verse declares that Jesus bore his name triumphantly on the cross and again in his resurrection. He was the human light who came into the world, according to John's Gospel, so that everyone who believes in him might not remain in darkness. He carried his name through the heavenly realms and all the invisible creatures which live in it to God's throne. As he himself states in John's Gospel, the word he spoke came from the Father. Since he came from God, once his mission on earth was complete, he returned to the Father's breast. And his name was filled with glory of the perfect rest he now enjoys at God's right hand.

The passage from the Acts of the Apostles narrates how the word of God continues to spread. By "word of God" is meant the preaching about the name of Jesus by his followers. Acts mentions Barnabas and Saul (Paul) and John Mark. However, there are other prophets and teachers in Antioch: Symeon (Niger), Lucius, and Manaen. While they are worshiping and fasting, they are told by the Holy Spirit to send Barnabas and Saul (Paul) on mission to other Gentiles. While they make it a point to announce the name of Jesus in Jewish synagogues, in which they are usually rejected, they turn to the Gentiles or the nations.

In so doing, Barnabas and Saul (Paul) fulfill a desire expressed in Psalm 67, namely, that God would let his way be known upon earth among all nations, and that he would offer his salvation to all peoples. The same Psalm expresses the desire that the Gentiles would be glad and exult in and praise Israel's God. This desire is fulfilled through the missionary work of Barnabas and, primarily, through Saul (Paul). And it is continued through our own missionary work today.

Meditation

In what specific ways are you a missionary to the nations?

Overcome with Paschal Joy

Prayer

LORD God, your Son, Jesus Christ, spread his message of salvation to his world and commissioned his followers to bring it to the nations. As his followers today, grant us the courage to proclaim it and the wisdom to understand it. On the other side of death, bring us the eternal light and glory in the heights of your kingdom, where Jesus lives and reigns with you and the Holy Spirit forever and ever. Amen.

Thursday of the Fourth Week of Easter

Scriptures
Acts 13:13–25;
John 13:16–20

Hymn
On Jordan's bank the Baptist's cry
Announces that the Lord is nigh;
Awake and harken, for he brings
Glad tidings of the King of kings.

"ON JORDAN'S BANK THE BAPTIST'S CRY," VERSE 1

Reflection: While many people associate "On Jordan's Bank the Baptist's Cry" with the Season of Advent, the first verse of the hymn also echoes Paul's words in the Acts of the Apostles on this Thursday of the Fourth Week of Easter. In a Jewish synagogue on the sabbath, Paul speaks by summarizing Hebrew and Israelite biblical history. The basic gist of his recounting is that God chose a people, led them out of Egyptian slavery into the desert for forty years, brought them to the promised land, gave them judges, then gave them kings—Saul and David—and brought to them a savior, Jesus.

Then, Paul mentions John the Baptist, who announced the Savior's coming by preaching a baptism of repentance on the banks of the Jordan River. John fulfilled the mission given to him, making sure that everyone understood that he was not the Savior; the one coming after him, the King of kings, whose sandals he was not worthy to unfasten, was the Messiah.

This is a summary of the first part of Paul's speech; the second part is the first Scripture text for tomorrow.

Even during the Easter Season, we remember John the Baptist. His role is to prepare people for the coming of the Lord. He does this by a re-orientation act, known as baptism. Water is a dual sign; it represents both death and life. Remember the great flood; in that story it represents death. Remember the story of the woman of Samaria at the well; in that story it represents life. Those who participate in John's baptism turn away or die to one way of life and turn toward or live a new way of life. As Paul makes clear in his speech, John's role is to be a step in God's plan just like Abraham, Jacob, Samuel, Saul, and David before him.

Meditation
What is your role in God's plan?
When you came to understand your role in God's plan,
was water involved in some way? How?

Prayer
Ever-living God, your servant John stood on the bank of the Jordan River and announced the coming of your Son into the world. With your Holy Spirit guide us to know our role in your plan. And when we have fulfilled it, grant us eternal life with the King of kings, Jesus Christ, who is Lord forever and ever. Amen.

Friday of the Fourth Week of Easter

Scriptures
Acts 13:26–33;
John 14:1–6

Hymn
Yet she on earth has union
With God, the Three in One,
And mystic sweet communion
With those whose rest is won.
O happy ones and holy!

Overcome with Paschal Joy

Lord, give us grace that we
Like them, the meek and lowly,
On high may dwell with thee.

"THE CHURCH'S ONE FOUNDATION," VERSE 4

Reflection: The "she" in verse four of "The Church's One Foundation" is the church; three aspects of her existence are given. First, the church is in union with the Triune God. Second, the church is composed of those who have died, and, third, of those who are still alive. Those who have not yet entered into eternal rest petition God to give them grace, that is, the gift of himself, so that they can enter into the realm of everlasting life where perfect communion between people and God exists.

The passage from John's Gospel portrays Jesus telling his disciples that in his Father's house there are many dwelling places. If Jesus were around today, he would speak about his Father's hotel or motel, the mystical church, in which there are more rooms than can be counted. Being a good innkeeper, he goes ahead of his disciples to get their rooms ready for their eternal rest. One day he will return to lead them to this dwelling on high.

Thomas does not understand the image of the church as at once here and forever eternal. So, he tells Jesus that he does not know where Jesus is going, and, therefore, he cannot know the way. This is the same Thomas who, at the end of the gospel, will need to see Jesus' wounds in order to believe that he has been raised from the dead. Thomas needs a road map or a GPS device in order to know the right direction to take. The Johannine Jesus reminds him that he is the way and the truth and the life. He is the road map or GPS that gets believers to the Father's motel. He speaks the truth about there being many rooms in his Father's hotel. And the eternal life of those who live there is given to them by Jesus. They share in all that now as members of the church; one day they will share in it forever.

Meditation
How does the church serve as the way, the truth, and the life for you now?

Fourth Week of Easter

Prayer

LORD God, Three in One, through the death and resurrection of your Son, our Lord Jesus Christ, you have established your church on earth and promised those who follow him an eternal dwelling place in your kingdom. Give us the grace to journey in your church below to that mystic communion of the saints in the eternal church, where you live as Father, Son, and Holy Spirit, forever and ever. Amen.

Saturday of the Fourth Week of Easter

Scriptures

Acts 13:44–52;
John 14:7–14

Hymn

Christians, this Lord Jesus
Shall return again,
With his Father's glory,
With his angel-train;
For all wreaths of empire
Meet upon his brow
And our hearts confess him
King of glory now.

"AT THE NAME OF JESUS," VERSE 8

Reflection: In John's Gospel, Jesus is the incarnate God. The Holy One became flesh in Jesus of Nazareth. Therefore, if a person knows Jesus, the person also knows the Father. If a person sees Jesus, the person also sees God. The Father is in Jesus, and Jesus is in the Father. The works Jesus does are the works of God. Those who believe in Jesus will be in him and be able to do the same works he does, because their faith in him will connect them to the Father through him. In other words, the Johannine Jesus is a living double entendre; he is simultaneously both the man Jesus and the divine

Christ (Father). Those who are connected to him humanly simultaneously have access to God's own life.

While this is not exactly the same message presented in the passage from the Acts of the Apostles, which is a continuation from yesterday's selection, it is similar. Paul and Barnabas rehearse for their audience the basic message about Jesus Christ: Because the Jews failed to recognize the salvation God was offering them, they handed over Jesus to Pilate, who had him crucified on a tree. After he died, he was buried in a tomb, from which God raised him from the dead. Today's passage picks up the rest of the story: The Jews contradict Paul's and Barnabas's message, which spurs them to turn to the Gentiles, who hear the word of God with joy, come to believe, and are destined for eternal life.

In the Synoptic Gospels of Mark, Matthew, and Luke, there is a hope that Jesus will return again with his Father's glory at some unknown time in the future. As verse eight of "At the Name of Jesus" states, the crowns of all world leaders will be placed on Christ's head because he will be king of glory. However, in John's Gospel, Jesus promises to send the Advocate (Paraclete) to continue to teach his disciples after he goes to the Father. The Advocate (Paraclete) is equated with the Holy Spirit in popular understanding, but he is a little different, too. The very name Jesus calls him indicates someone a little different. We will hear more about that Advocate (Paraclete) in next week's texts from John's Gospel.

Meditation

What is your hope for Jesus' return in glory?
Is it an event you expect to witness in your lifetime
or one to come at some indefinite time in the future?

Prayer

Lord Jesus, throughout the ages, your faithful followers have hoped for your return in your Father's glory. As we continue to celebrate your resurrection from the dead, strengthen our hope in this promise that we may join the angels and saints in confessing you as king of glory now and forever and ever. Amen.

12

Fifth Week of Easter

Fifth Sunday of Easter, Cycle A

Scriptures
Acts 6:1–7;
1 Peter 2:4–9;
John 14:1–12

Hymn
Name him, Christians, name him
With love as strong as death,
But with awe and wonder,
And with bated breath;
He is God the Savior,
He is Christ the Lord,
Ever to be worshiped,
Trusted, and adored.

"AT THE NAME OF JESUS," VERSE 7

Reflection: At this point in the Season of Easter, the daily Scripture texts and the Sunday Scripture texts are beginning to overlap. For example, earlier in the season we read today's passage from the Acts of the Apostles.

Overcome with Paschal Joy

And on last Friday and Saturday we read parts of today's passage from John's Gospel. The only selection for today that is new to us is the passage from the First Letter of Peter, a reflection on Jesus as the cornerstone, a living stone, and the stone rejected by the builders of a spiritual house. The basic metaphor meditated on by the author of the First Letter of Peter is, thus, stone. In a similar way, verse seven of "At the Name of Jesus" exhorts Christians to name Jesus "God the Savior" and "Christ the Lord."

When the author of the First Letter of Peter calls Jesus a living stone, he is referring to his resurrection from the dead. He is the living stone chosen and precious in God's sight. In the words of verse seven of "At the Name of Jesus," his love was as strong as death. All we can do is stand in awe and wonder with bated breath, recognizing that the risen Christ was made the cornerstone of a new temple, one Christians name church.

In order to aid the understanding of First Peter's meditation, it would be good to imagine a favorite stone building or to stand in front of one. From the outside, people see Jesus as a stone rejected by the builders, that is, he was tossed away like a stone that cannot be used in a building project. But to those who have faith, he is their solid rock, their cornerstone, which supports the whole church of believers. This makes them chosen, royal, holy, a people built into a spiritual house in which spiritual sacrifices are offered to God through Jesus Christ, who himself is worshiped, trusted, and adored. Because God raised Jesus from death to life, those stones who form his body (church) are living stones.

Meditation

What further depth have you discovered by reflecting on Jesus as the cornerstone, a living stone, and the stone rejected by the builders?

Prayer

God our Savior, with love as strong as death you raised your only-begotten Son from the tomb with awe and wonder on the third day and breathed into him the breath of life. As we come in worship of Christ the Lord, make us living stones and build us into your spiritual house on the cornerstone of him who is ever worshiped, trusted, and adored: our Lord Jesus Christ, who lives and reigns with you and the Holy Spirit, one God, forever and ever. Amen.

Fifth Week of Easter

Fifth Sunday of Easter, Cycle B

Scriptures
Acts 9:26–31;
1 John 3:18–24;
John 15:1–8

Hymn
But the pains which he endured, Alleluia!
Our salvation have procured; Alleluia!
Now exalted he is king, Alleluia!
Where the angels ever sing. Alleluia!

"JESUS CHRIST IS RISEN TODAY," VERSE 3

Reflection: Do pain and suffering lead to salvation? We don't associate pain with salvation, but verse three of "Jesus Christ Is Risen Today" does. The verse proposes that through pain one is healed. We presuppose that pain is to be eliminated through drugs, surgery, or psychological counseling. Salvation is joyful healing, feeling better; it is on the other side of pain. There is an oxymoronic character to the statement that through pain one is healed. This deep truth needs further exploration to access an understanding of it.

We begin with the good pain presented by the passage in today's unique reflection in John's Gospel. Employing the image of a vineyard filled with a grape vine and branches, Jesus states that every branch that bears good fruit is pruned by his Father so that it bears more fruit. This is a good pain, because it sparks more life. Any vineyard-owner knows that in order to get next year's harvest of grapes he must cut away this year's growth after this year's harvest. If the branches are not pruned, they will not bear fruit next year. Therefore, good pain (pruning) produces salvation (fruit).

Furthermore, life is dependent on the pruned branch, us, remaining on the vine, Jesus. The vine grower, God the Father, has made his only-begotten Son the true vine. Those who believe in him are growing branches to which he supplies all that keeps them alive and bearing fruit, even when the Father prunes them. The branches that are totally pruned because they do not bear fruit are cut off, wither, and are burned because they are useless, robbing the vine of valuable nutrients.

Meditation
How has your good pain led to abundant life?

Prayer
Vine-grower Father, you made your Son, Jesus Christ, the true vine of life for the branches of all believers. Fill us with his risen life that we can bear much fruit, exalt him as king, and glorify you. You are one God—Father, Son, and Holy Spirit—forever and ever. Amen.

Fifth Sunday of Easter, Cycle C

Scriptures
Acts 14:21–27;
Revelation 21:1–5a;
John 13:31–33a, 34–35

Hymn
At his voice creation
Sprang at once to light,
All the angel faces,
All the hosts of light,
Thrones and dominations,
Stars up on their way,
All the heav'nly orders
In their great array.

"AT THE NAME OF JESUS," VERSE 2

Reflection: The second verse of "At the Name of Jesus" reflects a Trinitarian understanding that God has always existed as three persons in one God.

Fifth Week of Easter

Thus, from the beginning of creation by God the Father, the voice of God the Son has been heard calling light and angels into existence. Likewise, the Holy Spirit has always been present breathing life into what the Father created through the voice of the Son. Such heavenly orders—archangels, angels, principalities, powers, virtues, dominations, thrones, cherubim, and seraphim—in their great array are collectively called the hosts of light because they serve the glory of God.

In the passage from John's Gospel, Jesus tells his disciples that he is being glorified and that God is glorified in him. Glory is oxymoronic in John's Gospel. Usually referring to God's revelation of himself as light, as seen throughout the Hebrew Bible (Old Testament) and in verse two of "At the Name of Jesus," in John's Gospel it is Jesus' passion, death, and resurrection that display God's light. In other words, what many people think of as darkness (passion and death) becomes glory (resurrection). God gives light to his Son, who has always shared his glory.

Glory is displayed in the passage from the Book of Revelation as a new heaven and a new earth, a new act of creation. The one who sits on the throne makes it very clear that he is making all things new. Thus, the new Jerusalem that comes from heaven is filled with light; she looks like a bride dressed in white and prepared to meet her groom. There is no need for the sun or moon—sources of light—because God dwells in the city. In other words, God's glory fills all with light.

Meditation
What have been your own experiences of God's glory (light)?

Prayer
From the beginning of time, Almighty God, the voice of your Son has called into existence the light of your glory. He glorified you through his death, and you glorified him through his resurrection. Glorify us with the Holy Spirit, who lives and reigns with you, Father, and our Lord Jesus Christ, one God, forever and ever. Amen.

Overcome with Paschal Joy

Monday of the Fifth Week of Easter

Scriptures
Acts 14:5–18;
John 14:21–26

Hymn
Easter triumph, Easter joy,
This alone can sin destroy;
From the death of sin set free:
Souls reborn, O Lord, we'll be.
Hymns of glory, songs of praise,
Father, unto you we raise;
And to you, our risen King,
With the Spirit, praise we sing.

"AT THE LAMB'S HIGH FEAST WE SING," VERSE 4

Reflection: The Easter triumph and Easter joy mentioned in verse four of "At the Lamb's High Feast We Sing" is displayed by Paul in the passage from the Acts of the Apostles. After traveling to the town of the Gentile city of Lystra, Paul (and Barnabas) encounters a crippled man, lame from birth. The astute reader will immediately recognize that this is the parallel story of Peter (and John) encountering a crippled man at an entrance to the temple in Jerusalem. Like Peter healed a crippled, Paul heals a cripple. This leads the crowd to conclude that their Gentile gods, Zeus and Hermes, have appeared in the persons of Barnabas and Paul. This leads Barnabas and Paul to proclaim the good news of the living God's latest deed, namely, Jesus' resurrection.

Sin destroys the new life of resurrection, but God has destroyed sin's death through the death and resurrection of Jesus Christ. Those who are reborn through baptism are set free from death and filled with Easter triumph and joy. In John's Gospel, this is known as love. Cultural love is not what is meant; in John's Gospel the word "love" means sacrifice, a life freely given away for another, as demonstrated in Jesus. Those who love him are loved by God, who reveals his love by raising his Son to new life and sending the Advocate to keep awakening sacrificial love in those Jesus has brought to God.

To these great acts of God only one response can be made. That response is to sing hymns of glory and songs of praise to the Father and to the risen king, Jesus Christ, in union with the Holy Spirit. In other words, all we can do is praise the Trinitarian God. This is what Barnabas and Paul told the Lycaonians, who wanted to offer sacrifice to them for healing the crippled man. They redirected the praise to the living God, who made heaven, earth, and sea—and all that is in each of them.

Meditation

For what great acts in your life do you need to praise God?

Prayer

You have brought the world Easter triumph and joy through the resurrection of our Lord Jesus Christ, ever-living God. His death destroyed death; through the water of baptism, we participate in his death and are reborn as your sons and daughters, O LORD. Accept our hymns of glory, our songs of praise, Father, which we raise to you through our risen king, your Son, who lives and reigns with you and the Holy Spirit, forever and ever. Amen.

Tuesday of the Fifth Week of Easter

Scriptures
Acts 14:19–28;
John 14:27–31a

Hymn
Alleluia! Alleluia! Alleluia!
The strife is o'er, the battle done.
The victory of life is won;
The song of triumph has begun: Alleluia!

"THE STRIFE IS O'ER, THE BATTLE DONE," REFRAIN AND VERSE 1

Overcome with Paschal Joy

Reflection: The word "strife" in the first verse of "The Strife Is O'er, the Battle Done," best summarizes the Scripture texts assigned for this Tuesday in the Fifth Week of Easter. Strife is found in the ongoing narrative of the missionary experiences of Paul and Barnabas in the Acts of the Apostles. Paul and Barnabas, according to the Acts, strengthened the spirits of the disciples they had made in three different Gentile cities, exhorting them to persevere in the faith. They said, "It is through many persecutions that we must enter the kingdom of God" (Acts 14:22). In other words, the earliest believers had to be willing to undergo much strife.

Strife also adequately describes the passage from John's Gospel. Before he leaves—through death and resurrection—Jesus tells his disciples not to be troubled or afraid. He gives his peace to them; this is not a peace in terms of the absence of war, but one which quiets them and removes their strife. He further calms them by telling them that while he is going away, he will return. In fact, their sacrificial love for him should be great enough to rejoice in his going to the Father.

We stand two thousand years after the disciples. Through his death and resurrection, Jesus has won the battle. The victory of eternal life has been given to us. Because he did his Father's will, we join him in singing the song of triumph. The daily strife of life is miniscule to the victory won. Jesus did not remove the strife that accompanies being human; he demonstrated how to beat it by doing God's will. As Paul and Barnabas tell the disciples they have gained, "It is through many persecutions that we must enter the kingdom of God" (Acts 14:22). If it were necessary in those days, it remains so today.

Meditation
What strife have you recently won and enjoyed the victory of life?

Prayer
Heavenly Father, in the battle between death and life, your Son won the victory of life. Grace us with your strength that our battles of earthly life may lead us to your kingdom. We sing the song of triumph to you, Father, who live and reign with our Lord Jesus Christ in the unity of the Holy Spirit, one God, forever and ever. Amen.

Fifth Week of Easter

Wednesday of the Fifth Week of Easter

Scriptures
Acts 15:1–6;
John 15:1–8

Hymn
Hymns of praise then let us sing, Alleluia!
Unto Christ, our heav'nly King, Alleluia!
Who endured the cross and grave, Alleluia!
Sinners to redeem and save. Alleluia!

"JESUS CHRIST IS RISEN TODAY," VERSE 2

Reflection: The narrative about the meeting in Jerusalem of the leaders of the church which is begun in today's passage from the Acts of the Apostles continues through Thursday and Friday. In the first segment today, we hear about some Judaizers who meet Paul and Barnabas and make it clear that circumcision is required of the Gentiles if they want to be saved. In other words, Gentile believers must become Jews first—since Jesus was Jewish—before they can become Christian. This, of course, caused great dissension and debate, especially among the male Gentiles! So, the leaders decide to go to Jerusalem and meet with other leaders to hear what they have to say about this issue. They had no more than entered the city when a party of Pharisees, who had become believers, made it clear that the circumcision of the Gentiles and observance of the law of Moses were required. Then, the meeting began.

The vine and branches analogy from John's Gospel is the same passage heard on the Fifth Sunday of Easter, Cycle B. Jesus compares the world to a vineyard owned and operated by the Father. The only vine is Jesus from whom all branches sprout. The Father prunes the branches in order to keep them bearing fruit. Every vineyard owner knows that the vines must be pruned after one harvest in order to insure next year's harvest. Branches that do not bear grapes are cut, piled, and burned. The analogy works as long as one knows a lot about viniculture.

Overcome with Paschal Joy

On this middle day of the Fifth Week of the Easter Season, facing the tough issues of our own day and time—drugs, alcohol, murder, abuse, etc.—the discussion about the circumcision of Gentiles pales in comparison. We do well to remember that Christ, our heavenly king, endured the cross and grave in order to redeem and save all sinners—circumcised or not! Once we see this larger picture, then we know that all we can do is sing hymns of praise to him.

Meditation
What is the toughest issue you face as a follower of Jesus Christ?

Prayer
Lord Jesus Christ, our heavenly king, you endured the cross and the tomb in order to redeem and save all people of the world. Give us a deeper appreciation for your sacrificial gift. Hear the hymns of praise we sing to you, who live and reign with the Father and the Holy Spirit, one God, forever and ever. Amen.

Thursday of the Fifth Week of Easter

Scriptures
Acts 15:7–21;
John 15:9–11

Hymn
In your hearts enthrone him;
There let him subdue
All that is not holy,
All that is not true;
Crown him as your captain
In temptation's hour;
Let his will enfold you
In its light and pow'r.

"AT THE NAME OF JESUS," VERSE 6

Fifth Week of Easter

Reflection: In the second part of the three-day series about the meeting of church leaders in Jerusalem, Peter tells the assembly that instead of debating whether or not the Gentiles should be circumcised, they should be thinking about how God has chosen them to hear the good news about Jesus of Nazareth, believe it, and receive the Holy Spirit. Instead of putting God to the test by their debate, they need to enthrone Jesus in their hearts, where he can subdue this Jewish desire which is not holy. The truth is that the Gentiles are saved through the grace of the Lord Jesus in the same way as the Jews. Peter puts both Jews and Gentiles on the same level field, declaring that all need to be saved.

However, it is James who expresses the opinion that in this hour of temptation the assembly should stop troubling the Gentiles who have crowned Jesus as their captain. Through Christ, God has enfolded them in his light and power, and they need only to avoid idols, unlawful marriage, the meat of strangled animals, and blood. These requirements, which do not include circumcision, distill a basic way of life free from all gods except the LORD, free from fornication, eating only creatures killed according to kosher laws, and not eating blood, which belonged to God because ancient people thought that life was in the blood. These basic practices are to be observed so as not to give offense to Jewish Christians.

The Jerusalem assembly, as voiced by James, sees a broad world where Jews and Gentiles live together in harmony. In John's Gospel, Jesus refers to this as love, specifically sacrificial love. One's personal desire is sacrificed for the common good. What is good for the whole is put ahead of what is good for the individual. This is where United States culture with its emphasis on the individual collides with biblical culture and its emphasis on the common good. There is room for compromise. While the Pharisees want the Gentiles to be circumcised, the leaders decide that practice is too radical; they adopt a compromise position in order to bring together under the one God two different groups needing salvation: Jews and Gentiles.

Meditation

Upon what issues today can you apply the common good principle?
What change will that require of you?

Overcome with Paschal Joy

Prayer

Lord Jesus Christ, your love for people was so great that you sacrificed your life to show them how to live together in peace. Come and be enthroned in our hearts, and there subdue all that is not holy, all that is not true. When we are tempted with selfishness, enfold us with the light and power of the common good. You live and reign with the Father and the Holy Spirit, one God, forever and ever. Amen.

Friday of the Fifth Week of Easter

Scriptures

Acts 15:22–31;
John 15:12–17

Hymn

Sing we to our God above, Alleluia!
Praise eternal as his love; Alleluia!
Praise him, all you heav'nly host, Alleluia!
Father, Son, and Holy Ghost. Alleluia!

"JESUS CHRIST IS RISEN TODAY," VERSE 4

Reflection: The passage from the Acts of the Apostles is the last of the three sections narrating the meeting in Jerusalem. Once the church leaders have made their decision about the Gentiles not needing to be circumcised, they choose men to send to the Gentiles with a letter informing them of their decision. The letter makes it clear that it is the decision of the Holy Spirit and of the leaders not to place any burdens on the Gentiles, except to abstain from meat sacrificed to idols because it will look like they are worshiping idols; to abstain from blood, since all blood belongs to God; to abstain from meats of strangled animals, because they have not been slaughtered in a humane manner; and to abstain from fornication. Those who received the letter were delighted with it. Especially the Gentile men were singing to God above!

John's Gospel presents Jesus' reflections on friendship. A friend is someone who is emotionally close to another, sharing mutual affection and trust. The Johannine Jesus calls this love. The greatest love that one can demonstrate is laying down one's life for one's friend. Jesus tells his disciples that he calls them his friends because they are sharing his affection for and trust of them. He adds the fact that they did not choose him as a friend; he chose them to bear fruit. Then, he tells them that his command is for them to love one another as he loves them. This is a type of passing on of friendship.

In an age when people spend more time trying to manipulate others so they can get what they want, Jesus' reflections on true or authentic friendship serve as an antidote to fake relationships. While it may never be necessary for one friend to die for another, many opportunities present themselves for one friend to demonstrate his or her sacrificial love for another. In a rushed age, maybe just giving time to be with the beloved is sacrifice enough. Certainly, taking a walk together, sharing a meal together, or going to a movie together strengthens the bond of friendship. Such practices, which require sacrificial love, bear fruit. They usually free the two friends to reach outward to others and bring them into the realm of their love.

Meditation

Who is your best friend?
What do the two of you do to strengthen your love for each other?
How does that love reach outward to others?

Prayer

We praise your eternal love, almighty God, as we sing praise to your name. Through our Lord Jesus Christ, you have taught us the deeper meaning of sacrificial love in friendship. Through our Lord Jesus Christ, you have revealed how one can die for a friend. Send us authentic friends, who join us in praising you, Father, Son, and Holy Spirit, forever and ever. Amen.

Overcome with Paschal Joy

Saturday of the Fifth Week of Easter

Scriptures
Acts 16:1–10;
John 15:18–21

Hymn
Still for us he intercedes, Alleluia!
His prevailing death he pleads, Alleluia!
Near himself prepares our place, Alleluia!
He the first fruits of our race, Alleluia!

"HAIL THE DAY THAT SEES HIM RISE," VERSE 5

Reflection: On this last day of the Fifth Week of Easter, verse five of "Hail the Day That Sees Him Rise" informs us that Jesus still intercedes for us with God. An intercessor is one who pleads on another's behalf. According to the verse of the hymn, it is his death on the cross that pleads to God on behalf of all people. Because he is the first fruits, that is, the firstborn from the dead of our race, he has prepared a dwelling place for us in his Father's house.

The passage from the Acts of the Apostles presents Paul's companion, Timothy. Those who know this disciple intercede for him with Paul, who has him circumcised before he joins the mission journey from one city to another. Another intercession occurs when the text states that the Spirit of Jesus kept Paul and Timothy from traveling to Bithynia. And a third intercession occurs when Paul has a vision; the vision sends him to Macedonia to proclaim the good news to people there. In the very last verse of today's passage, there is a shift from third-person narrative to first-person narrative. The author, who has been telling the story in third person, suddenly states, "... God had called us ..." (Acts 16:10), a shift to first-person narrative. From this point on the author seems to draw from journal entries to record the spread of the gospel. Biblical scholars call these "we passages" because, like tomorrow's story from the Acts, they begin with the word "we." In other words, the biblical author intercedes with the journal's author for some of his material.

Fifth Week of Easter

In John's Gospel, Jesus is presented as an intercessor for his followers. He tells them that the world will hate them, just as it has hated him. They no longer belong to the world because he has chosen them out of the world, and the world hates those who have been chosen to do great things. The world will persecute them for the words they speak. However, while they are hated and persecuted, Jesus will be with them, interceding for them.

Meditation
Who has served as an intercessor for you? For whom have you interceded?

Prayer
Lord Jesus, through your resurrection from the dead, you became the first fruits of our race and prepared a place for us in the kingdom of God. As we spread your gospel to all we meet, continue to intercede for us with the Father, who lives and reigns with you and the Holy Spirit, one God, forever and ever. Amen.

13

Sixth Week of Easter

When the Solemnity of the Ascension of the Lord is celebrated next Sunday, the second reading and gospel from the Seventh Sunday of Easter in all three cycles may be read on the Sixth Sunday of Easter. Entries for the Seventh Sunday of Easter can be found at the back of this book.

Sixth Sunday of Easter, Cycle A

Scriptures
Acts 8:5–8, 14–17;
1 Peter 3:15–18;
John 14:15–21

Hymn
Come, holy Comforter,
Your sacred witness bear
In this glad hour!
Your grace to us impart,
Now rule in ev'ry heart,
Never from us depart,
Spirit of pow'r.

"COME, OUR ALMIGHTY KING," VERSE 3

Sixth Week of Easter

Reflection: Verse three of "Come, Our Almighty King," is a prayer invoking the presence of the Holy Spirit, the Comforter (Advocate, Paraclete), and seeking his grace, rule, presence, and power. Grace refers to God's gift of himself to people, commonly personified as the Holy Spirit. Rule refers to submission to God which begins in one's heart. Knowing the abiding but unseen presence of God is another way to speak about the Holy Spirit. And power in mighty deeds is what God is able to do through the person he graces, rules, and lavishes with his presence. Jesus addresses these in the passage from John's Gospel. He tells his disciples that the Father will grace them with the Advocate, who will guide or rule them, who will be with them always, and who will fill them with powerful truth.

The story about Philip's success in Samaria is another account of the presence and work of the Holy Spirit. Through Philip, the Spirit casts out unclean spirits, heals paralyzed and crippled people, and fills people with great joy. As a result, many are baptized in the name of the Lord Jesus. Then, Peter and John arrive in Samaria and lay hands on the heads of Philip's converts. They received the same Holy Spirit who had been at work in Philip's deeds among them.

The passage from the First Letter of St. Peter presents the work of the Holy Spirit in the life of Jesus. After he was put to death in the flesh on the cross, he was brought to life in the Spirit. The Holy Spirit is like an energy that cannot be contained; it is like an unseen force that can be felt or sensed; it is like the essence of life that pervades and unites all.

Meditation
How do you describe your experiences of the Holy Spirit?

Prayer
Come, Holy Comforter, and impart your grace to your people. Strengthen us to bear witness to the death and resurrection of Jesus Christ. Grant that we may know your abiding and healing presence in our lives. You live and rule, Advocate, with the Father and the Son, one God, forever and ever. Amen.

Overcome with Paschal Joy

Sixth Sunday of Easter, Cycle B

Scriptures
Acts 10:25–26, 34–35, 44–48;
1 John 4:7–10;
John 15:9–17

Hymn
Come, our almighty King,
Help us your name to sing;
Help us to praise:
Father, all glorious,
Ever victorious,
Come and reign over us,
Ancient of Days.

"COME, OUR ALMIGHTY KING," VERSE 1

Reflection: The passage from the Acts of the Apostles is an edited version of a much longer story found in the second volume of Luke-Acts. It begins with Peter's vision and Cornelius's vision. Cornelius, a Roman, Gentile military commander, sends men to Peter, and Peter follows them to the commander's home. He tells Cornelius and his whole household about the death and resurrection of Jesus, and they become believers. This leads Peter to make this famous announcement: "I truly understand that God shows no partiality, but in every nation anyone who fears him and does what is right is acceptable to him" (Acts 10:34–35). This is quite an extraordinary statement for a Jew to make about a Gentile!

Another extraordinary thing occurs: While Peter speaks, the Holy Spirit descends on Cornelius, his household, and anyone else listening to the word. This leads those Jews who had accompanied Peter to be astounded that the gift of the Holy Spirit should be given to the Gentiles. Then, Peter calls for water and baptizes everyone in the name of Jesus Christ. Here, the reader should note that instead of baptism and then the Holy Spirit, it is the Holy Spirit followed by baptism.

Sixth Week of Easter

Both the passage from the First Letter of John and John's Gospel proclaim that God is love. Because God is love, he loves us first. He demonstrates his love by sending his only Son into the world. God's love is self-sacrificial; he gives himself to people because that is his essence. Jesus tells his disciples to pass on God's love. Just as the Father loves Jesus, so Jesus loves his followers, who are commanded to love one another just as Jesus loves them: self-sacrificially. This kind of love is what Jewish Peter demonstrates by entering Gentile Cornelius's home and discovering that God shows no partiality; God loves all people, Jews and Gentiles, and offers them life through his Son, Jesus Christ.

Meditation

How have you experienced God's love for you?
Was it through Jesus or some other way?
What was the insight you gained
that propelled you into even deeper love for God, Jesus, and others?

Prayer

Lord Jesus, you are God's messenger of eternal love. This Sunday give us voice to praise your name; to praise the name of your glorious and victorious Father, the Ancient of Days; and to praise the name of your life-giving Holy Spirit. With the Father and the Holy Spirit you live and abide in love, forever and ever. Amen.

Sixth Sunday of Easter, Cycle C

Scriptures

Acts 15:1–2, 22–29;
Revelation 21:10–14, 22–23;
John 14:23–29

Hymn

Come, O incarnate Word,
Gird on your mighty sword;

Overcome with Paschal Joy

> Our prayer attend:
> Come and your people bless,
> And give your word success;
> Spirit of holiness,
> On us descend.
>
> "COME, OUR ALMIGHTY KING," VERSE 2

Reflection: At this point in the Easter Season the weekday Scriptures texts are overlapping with the Sunday Scripture texts. For example, today's Acts narrative about the meeting in Jerusalem of the leaders of the church to discuss whether or not Gentiles had to be circumcised was read in its longer form on Wednesday, Thursday, and Friday of the Fifth Week of Easter. The passage from John's Gospel assigned for today was read in a longer form on Tuesday of the Fifth Week of Easter. Thus, we will reflect on the passage from the Book of Revelation.

Bidding the incarnate Word, Jesus Christ, to come and gird on his mighty sword occurred earlier in this last book of the Bible. Once all evil has been defeated John of Patmos, the seer, witnesses the new holy city Jerusalem coming down out of heaven from God, who has attended the prayer of his people, destroyed all evil, and is blessing his people with a new, splendorous creation. The city's basic structure is based on the number twelve (twelve tribes of Israel, twelve apostles; twelve is the sum of seven, completion [three, the number for God, plus four, the number for the earth], plus five, the first five books of the Bible known as the Pentateuch).

The perfectly cubed city has twelve gates, three in each of four walls facing in each of the four cardinal directions, upon which are written the names of the twelve tribes of Israel, Jacob's twelve sons. Each wall is built with twelve courses of stones to represent the twelve apostles of the Lamb, the incarnate Word in John's Gospel. The reader should be aware that mythological types—deep structures of meaning—are being used here. There were never twelve tribes of Israel, because Joseph was never a tribe. If one notices that there is a half tribe of Manasseh and a half tribe of Ephraim, the total reaches thirteen tribes! The same is true for the twelve apostles; besides the twelve that Jesus chose—and the lists of names differ slightly from one gospel to the next—there is Matthias in the Acts of the Apostles and Paul, who names himself an apostle, and Barnabas, who works with

Paul for a while. So, the minimum number of apostles, not counting the variants in the lists of them in the gospels, is fifteen! Knowing these facts does not diminish the truth that the author of Revelation is attempting to disclose, namely, that the new Jerusalem is built on the foundation of Jews and Christians. It has no temple because God and the Lamb live in it; thus, the whole city is a temple. Likewise, there is no sun or moon to shine on it, because God gives it light, and the Lamb is its lamp.

In the words of verse two of "Come, Our Almighty King," the incarnate Word, the Lamb, has come and blessed his people. Not only has his word and those to whom he entrusted it been successful, but those chosen by God in the past to deliver the LORD's word have been successful. Now, the Spirit of holiness, whom Jesus calls the Advocate in John's Gospel, has descended upon the world, like the city descending from the heavens.

Meditation

What newness has descended upon you this Easter Season?
What numbers are special to you?
What is the deeper meaning of those numbers?

Prayer

LORD God, you have mercy on your people and you bless them from one end of the earth to the other. Your greatest blessing was your incarnate Word, Jesus Christ, who, through his death and resurrection, defeated evil and brought new life to your people. Hear our prayers this day and make your word fruitful within us by the descent of the Spirit of holiness into our hearts. We ask this through our Lamb, who lives and reigns with you and the Advocate, one God, forever and ever. Amen.

Monday of the Sixth Week of Easter

Scriptures

Acts 16:11–15;
John 15:26–16:4a

Overcome with Paschal Joy

Hymn
Jesus Christ is ris'n today, Alleluia!
Our triumphant holy day, Alleluia!
Who did once upon the cross, Alleluia!
Suffer to redeem our loss. Alleluia!

"JESUS CHRIST IS RISEN TODAY," VERSE 1

Reflection: The Sixth Week of Easter might appropriately also be named "Spirit week" because most of the Scripture texts are about the sending or work of the Holy Spirit. In the passage from the Acts of the Apostles, Paul and Silas make their way to Philippi, where they find a place of prayer for women. They meet Lydia, a dealer in expensive purple cloth and a worshiper of God, who opens her heart to listen to Paul. After the Spirit moves her to understand Paul's message, she is baptized.

In part of his farewell speech to his disciples, the Johannine Jesus tells them that the Advocate, the Spirit of truth who proceeds from the Father, will be sent to them. He will testify, that is, bear witness, to Jesus. And once his disciples have received him, they, too, will testify to Jesus. The result of their testimony will be suffering: expulsion from synagogues and death.

In other words, those who follow Jesus have the cross and resurrection of Jesus traced in their lives. The one who once suffered on the cross to redeem the human race was raised triumphantly from the dead. His disciples should expect that what happened to him will happen to them, maybe not to the same degree, but, nevertheless, suffering will be a part of their lives. In the midst of suffering, God sends the Advocate both to remind them of Jesus and to enable them to bear witness to his death and resurrection. Every time a follower of Christ passes through some type of suffering, he or she can testify that Jesus Christ is raised in him or her.

Meditation
What suffering and new life has led you to recognize
that the cross and resurrection of Jesus is being traced in your life?
How did the Holy Spirit help you to bear witness to this?

Sixth Week of Easter

Prayer

Ever-living God, on the cross your Son, our Lord Jesus Christ, suffered to redeem the human race. On the third day your raised him triumphantly. As you trace his suffering and new life in us, his followers, strengthen our testimony with the gift of your Holy Spirit, who lives and reigns with you and the same Jesus Christ, one God, forever and ever. Amen.

Tuesday of the Sixth Week of Easter

Scriptures
Acts 16:22–34;
John16:5–11

Hymn
Holy, Holy, Holy! Lord God Almighty!
Early in the morning our song shall rise to thee:
Holy, Holy, Holy! Merciful and mighty,
God in three Persons, blessed Trinity.

"HOLY, HOLY, HOLY!" VERSE 1

Reflection: According to the story about Paul and Silas in the passage from the Acts of the Apostles, it was midnight—early in the morning—when they were singing hymns to God and an earthquake occurred, causing the foundations of the jail to shake, the prison doors to fly open, and their chains to be pulled loose. The earthquake, of course, is a theophany, a manifestation of God. In ancient cosmology, the only one who can shake the seven pillars upon which the plate-like surface of the earth rests is the LORD God Almighty.

The jailer, who has been asleep, witnesses the effects of the theophany and concludes that he might as well take his own life because his boss will take it when he finds out that the prisoners have escaped. His interpretation of the theophany is changed by Paul and Silas, who have not left the prison. In fact, the jailer shines a light on them which means that he is now ready to believe. Paul and Silas tell him about the death and resurrection of Jesus. He takes them to his home to spread the light to his whole household during the darkness of early morning. The jailer and his family are baptized, and then all share a meal together, rejoicing in their faith in the merciful and mighty God.

    In his lengthy farewell speech in John's Gospel, Jesus explains to his disciples that he is returning to God from whom he came. Once he goes to God he will send them the Advocate, who will reveal even more truth to them. Only in John's Gospel do we find the word "Advocate," sometimes translated as "Paraclete." The theophany that will occur once Jesus dies, is raised, and returns to the Father will be mighty assistance or help. This Helper has been equated with the theophanic appearance of the Holy Spirit breathed upon the disciples by Jesus on Easter Sunday evening. While always being one of the three persons in the one God, the Holy Spirit is intensified in John's Gospel; he is the Spirit of truth, who opens the minds of the disciples, who bears witness to Jesus, who reveals the world's errors, and gives glory to Jesus. In other words, wherever he is present there is an earthquake!

Meditation

What theophanic signs of the Spirit's presence have you experienced?

Prayer

LORD God Almighty, you are indeed holy! Hear our song of praise this day and reveal yourself to all who sing to you. Merciful and mighty One, you are God in three Persons, blessed Trinity, forever and ever. Amen.

Wednesday of the Sixth Week of Easter

Scriptures
Acts 17:15, 22–18:1;
John 16:12–15

Hymn
Alleluia! Alleluia! Alleluia!
On the third morn he rose again

Sixth Week of Easter

Glorious in majesty to reign;
O let us swell the joyful strain: Alleluia!

"THE STRIFE IS O'ER, THE BATTLE DONE," REFRAIN AND VERSE 3

Reflection: The refrain and third verse of "The Strife is O'er, the Battle Done," accurately summarizes Paul's speech to the Athenians found in today's passage from the Acts of the Apostles. As he walks through Athens, Paul notices the religiosity of the Athenians; they have many shrines to many gods. They even have a shrine "To an Unknown God" to be sure that they have paid homage to all gods. Paul uses the altar dedicated to this unknown god as his launching pad to explain who that god is.

Paul tells the Athenians that the unknown god is the God who created the heavens and the earth, who created people and breathed life into them, who created order out of chaos. According to Paul, instead of looking outside for God or creating some image of him, people should look inside; in him they live and move and have their being. This God has given the Gentiles an opportunity to repent through the man he appointed and confirmed by resurrection from the dead: Jesus.

The topic of resurrection from the dead is near and dear to the Greeks. In a part of the story omitted from today's passage, Paul enters into discussion with the Greek philosophers. Then, he goes to the Areopagus, where Athenian trials are held. And, like a lawyer defending his client, Paul presents his case to the Athenians. Basically, Paul presents enough evidence to convince some listeners that they now can know the unknown god and change their minds. This God has been revealed to them through the resurrection of Jesus. Some believe Paul, but more prefer to hear more about the resurrection from the dead at another time.

Meditation
What does the phrase "resurrection from the dead" mean to you?

Prayer
Creator God, after making the world and all that is in it you formed people and breathed into them the breath of life. As we have come to know that in you we

live and move and have our being, we have also come to believe that you raised your Son from the dead on the third morning after his crucifixion, restoring his life and seating him in majesty to reign at your right hand. Deepen your Spirit of truth in us and hear our joyful strain of praise through the same Jesus Christ our Lord. Amen.

Thursday of the Sixth Week of Easter

If today is the Solemnity of the Ascension, go to chapter 14 and omit today's exercise. If the Ascension is transferred to the Seventh Sunday of Easter (next Sunday), use the following exercise.

Scriptures
Acts 18:1–8;
John 16:16–20

Hymn
Alleluia! Not as orphans
Are we left in sorrow now;
Alleluia! He is near us,
Faith believes, nor questions how:
Though the cloud from sight received him,
When the forty days were o'er.
Shall our hearts forget his promise,
"I am with you evermore"?

"ALLELUIA! SING TO JESUS!" VERSE 2

Reflection: As the second verse of "Alleluia! Sing to Jesus!" states, this is the fortieth day of Easter. In a few places, this day is Ascension Thursday when, according to the Acts of the Apostles, Jesus was lifted up from the earth and a cloud took him from the sight of his disciples. In most places, Ascension is celebrated this coming Sunday. If today is the Solemnity of the Ascension where you live, then skip ahead and use the proper reflection. If Ascension

Sixth Week of Easter

is marked on Sunday, stay where you are. For those who celebrate Ascension today and the Seventh Sunday of Easter on Sunday, the reflections for Ascension can be found at the beginning of chapter 14; the reflections for the Seventh Sunday of Easter can be found at the back of this book.

The second verse of "Alleluia! Sing to Jesus!" also echoes the passage from John's Gospel. In his farewell discourse, Jesus explains to his disciples that in a little while they will no longer see him because he will be crucified. Then, a little while later they will see him because God will raise him from the dead. After he returns to the Father, from whom he came, he will not leave them as orphans; he will send them the Holy Spirit, who will comfort them in their grief. Even though it will look like he is gone, he will be with them forever. Something new is stirring in the world!

Likewise, there is something new stirring in the passage from the Acts of the Apostles. Silas, Timothy, and Paul make their way to Corinth, where Paul preaches to the Jews that the anointed one, that is, the Christ or the Messiah, was Jesus. When they do not listen, he turns his attention to the Gentiles. Many Gentiles hear, believe, and are baptized. The Christ (Greek for "anointed"), the Messiah (Hebrew for "anointed"), awaited by Jews is rejected by his own people, but he is accepted by Gentiles. How's that for something new?!

Meditation

What new stirring is occurring in your life during this Easter Season?

Prayer

Father, you have revealed to the nations of the world your saving power in the resurrection and ascension of your Son. Grant us the grace to learn the truth that out of suffering and death come new life and joy. We ask this in the name of Jesus Christ, who lives and reigns with you and the Holy Spirit, one God, forever and ever. Amen.

Friday of the Sixth Week of Easter

Scriptures
Acts 18:9–18;
John 16:20–23

Overcome with Paschal Joy

Hymn

Holy, Holy, Holy! Though the darkness hide thee,
Though the eye made blind by sin thy glory may not see,
Only thou art holy; there is none beside thee,
Perfect in pow'r, in love, and purity.

"HOLY, HOLY, HOLY!" VERSE 3

Reflection: The word "holy" means "separate." Almighty God is separate from the people he created. The third verse of "Holy, Holy, Holy!" illustrates the separateness of God; he is hidden in the darkness (or lightness) of the cloud. Throughout the Bible, no person can see God and live because people are blinded by sin. Only God is holy; only God is divine; he has no equal. He is perfect or all-powerful, all-loving, all-pure.

This understanding of holiness underlies the passage from the Acts of the Apostles, which narrates a vision Paul has of God while he is in Corinth. A vision is some type of ecstatic experience, a medium of God's revelation to people, through sign or word or both. In Paul's case, the vision is in word. God tells the apostle not to be afraid, but to go on speaking about Jesus. Because God is with Paul, no harm will come to him. Indeed, God has many people in Corinth who belong to him, that is, through their belief in Paul's preaching about Jesus Christ, they share in God's holiness, God's divinity, in whatever degree God enables people to do so.

In Jesus' farewell discourse in John's Gospel, from which today's passage is taken, Jesus employs the image of a woman in labor. When the time arrives for a pregnant woman to give birth, she goes into labor or anguish. Once she has given birth, according to Jesus, joy overwhelms her because her child has been born into the world. God brings about holiness in us in just this way. Belief in Jesus' resurrection is the conception of holiness. After this belief gestates and grows we give birth to deeper faith which usually involves some kind of grieving for the passing of a former way of life. However, the new way of life gives us a joy that no one can take away. That is holiness; that is a sharing in the very divinity of God.

Sixth Week of Easter

Meditation
What is your degree of holiness?
What have you relinquished in order to get to where you are now in relationship with God?

Prayer
LORD, Most High, you are the awesome, the great king over all the earth. Through the death and resurrection of your Son, Jesus Christ, you have poured your holiness on people and revealed your power, love, and purity. Hear our praises this day: Holy, holy, holy are you, Father, with your Son and the Holy Spirit forever and ever. Amen.

Saturday of the Sixth Week of Easter

Scriptures
Acts 18:23–28;
John 16:23b–28

Hymn
Alleluia! King eternal,
You the Lord of lords we own;
Alleluia! born of Mary,
Earth your footstool, heav'n your throne.
You within the veil have entered,
Robed in flesh, our great high priest;
You on earth both priest and victim
In the eucharistic feast.

"ALLELUIA! SING TO JESUS!" VERSE 4

Reflection: In verse four of "Alleluia! Sing to Jesus!" the risen Christ is hailed as God is in Psalm 47, today's Responsorial Psalm (47:2-3, 8-9, 10). The LORD is the great king of the whole earth, reigning over all nations, sitting upon his throne. God's attributes are applied to Jesus. After his resurrection, he is the eternal king, the Lord of lords, born of Mary. As he sits upon his heavenly throne, the earth serves as his footstool. The kingly imagery reaches a crescendo on the last Sunday of every liturgical year called the Solemnity of Our Lord Jesus Christ, King of the Universe. In today's passage from John's Gospel, the image of God as king and Jesus sitting on his right hand is presumed. The Johannine Jesus tells his disciples that they can ask the Father for anything in his name, and God will give it to them because they believe in the only Son of God. In other words, the King will grant requests made in the name of his Son.

The verse of the hymn changes imagery with line five when it declares that Christ has entered behind the veil of the holy of holies, the innermost part of the temple into which the high priest entered but once a year to seek atonement for the sins of the people. Using language and imagery from the Letter to the Hebrews, the hymn declares that Jesus, the man robed in human flesh, born of Mary, has entered the eternal temple where God lives in heaven as the final and greatest high priest, who offered himself to God once for all. Thus, when Christians celebrate the eucharist, Christ serves as priest in the person of the minister, as sacrificial victim under the forms of bread and wine, and, in one of the Easter Prefaces, as the altar upon whom he offers himself as the lamb of sacrifice.

None of this lofty and deep theological language can be found in today's Scriptures texts because it did not yet exist when these readings were written near the end of the first century CE. What is found in today's texts is a short narrative about the origin of one of Paul's companions: Apollos, a native of Alexandria, an authority on the Hebrew Scriptures (Old Testament). Apollos used the Hebrew Bible (Old Testament) to establish that the anointed one (Messiah [Hebrew], the Christ [Greek]) is Jesus. Apollos had been instructed in the Way of the Lord, one of the first names for what later became Christianity, and he learned more about it from two other Pauline associates: Priscilla and Aquila. As a catechist, Apollos instructed others in the Way.

Meditation
Who have been your catechists, namely,
those who have instructed you in the Way to live your faith?

Sixth Week of Easter

Prayer

Jesus Christ, you are the Lord of lords and King of kings, enthroned at your Father's right hand, using the earth as your footstool. After becoming man in the womb of your mother, Mary, you, high priest, offered yourself as the victim on the altar of the cross to save us. As we share the eucharistic feast of your body and blood, we participate in your great sacrifice. Grant that this food will nourish us on our journey to your Father's kingdom, where you live and reign with the Holy Spirit, one God, forever and ever. Amen.

14

Seventh Week of Easter

If the Solemnity of the Ascension was celebrated on Thursday of the Sixth Week of Easter, use the exercise for the Seventh Sunday of Easter found at the back of this book.

Solemnity of the Ascension of the Lord, Cycle A

Scriptures
Acts 1:1–11;
Ephesians 1:17–23;
Matthew 28:16–20

Hymn
See, he lifts his hands above, Alleluia!
See, he shows the prints of love, Alleluia!
Hark, his gracious lips bestow, Alleluia!
Blessing on his Church below. Alleluia!

"HAIL THE DAY THAT SEES HIM RISE," VERSE 4

Reflection: The ascension of the risen Christ has three different meanings in the three Scripture texts assigned for this solemnity. The passage from the Acts of the Apostles presumes a three-storied universe: heaven above, earth in the middle, the underworld below. The Jesus who came from heaven to earth now returns to heaven with the promise to come again. This is echoed in verse four of "Hail the Day That Sees Him Rise" when the words state he lifts his hands while rising from the earth and shows the nail prints of the cross.

The author of the Letter to the Ephesians understands ascension as Christ's enthronement in heaven at God's right hand, putting everything under his authority, and making him the head of the church, which is also his body on earth. This is echoed in verse four of "Hail the Day That Sees Him Rise" when the words state that he utters words of blessing on his church on earth.

Curiously, the passage from the very end of Matthew's Gospel is not about ascension at all. Jesus appears to the remaining eleven disciples (Judas has committed suicide) and commissions them to go to the nations, that is, the Gentiles, and baptize. His final words in Matthew's Gospel to his disciples are these: ". . . I am with you always, to the end of the age" (Matt 28:20). In other words, Jesus does not disappear from the earth; wherever two or three gather in his name, he is in their midst.

Meditation
Which meaning of the ascension gets most of your attention?
How can you apply that to your new life in Christ?

Prayer
LORD, Most High, you are the great king over all the earth. On this day we sing hymns of praise to your Son, our Lord Jesus Christ, seated at your right hand. As we await his return in glory, make us bearers of the good news of his death, resurrection, and ascension. We ask this through the same Jesus Christ, who lives and reigns with you and the Holy Spirit, one God, forever and ever. Amen.

Solemnity of the Ascension of the Lord, Cycle B

Scriptures
Acts 1:1–11;
Ephesians 1:17–23 or 4:1–13;
Mark 16:15–20

Overcome with Paschal Joy

Hymn

Highest heav'n its Lord receives, Alleluia!
Yet he loves the earth he leaves; Alleluia!
Though returning to his throne, Alleluia!
Still he calls us all his own. Alleluia!

"HAIL THE DAY THAT SEES HIM RISE," VERSE 3

Reflection: The ascension of the risen Christ is presented with three different meanings by each of the three Scripture texts assigned for this solemnity. The passage from the Acts of the Apostles presumes a three-storied universe: heaven above, earth in the middle, the underworld below. The Jesus who came from heaven to earth now returns to the highest heaven while still loving the earth from which he is departing. This is echoed in verse three of "Hail the Day That Sees Him Rise" when the words state he returns to his throne while still claiming his followers as his own.

The first option of a text from the Letter to the Ephesians is the same as in the Cycle A set of Scripture texts; it depicts the enthronement of Christ at God's right hand. The second option also focuses on the risen Christ enthroned. However, it explains that the one who ascended also descended from the heaven to the earth. The one who descended is also the one who ascended so that he might fill all things with his risen life. Those believers on earth he established as his body, the members of whom have various roles and responsibilities, keep growing to maturity to the extent of the full stature of Christ.

The third meaning of the ascension is found in the passage from Mark's Gospel. It is taken from what is known as the longer or third ending of Mark. Yes, Mark's Gospel has the original ending at 16:8, a shorter ending added to 16:8, and a longer ending at 16:9–20. This portion of the longer ending is chosen to emphasize the missionary aspect of the ascension. As stated in the Acts passage, where the two men dressed in white garments ask the apostles why they are looking at the sky—implying that they need to get busy with their mission of witnessing to the death and resurrection of Jesus—in the longer ending of Mark's Gospel Jesus sends his disciples with the message of the good news to every creature, promising them accompanying signs. The narrator states that he was then taken up to heaven at his seat at the right hand of God while he worked with them.

Seventh Week of Easter

Meditation

Which meaning of the ascension gets most of your attention? How can you apply that to your new life in Christ?

Prayer

God and Father of all, you are over all and through all and in all. You bestow your grace to each person according to the measure of Christ's gift of apostles, prophets, evangelists, pastors, and teachers to your church. Through your Holy Spirit, you build up the body of Christ and are constantly at work bringing her to the full stature of Christ. Keep us in the bond of peace; keep us faithful to the one hope of our call. You are one God, who lives and reigns with our one Lord, Jesus Christ, in the unity of the one Holy Spirit, forever and ever. Amen.

Solemnity of the Ascension of the Lord, Cycle C

Scriptures

Acts 1:1–11;
Ephesians 1:17–23 or Hebrews 9:24–28; 10:19–23;
Luke 24:46–53

Hymn

Hail the day that sees him rise, Alleluia!
To his throne above the skies; Alleluia!
Christ awhile to mortals giv'n, Alleluia!
Reascends his native heav'n. Alleluia!

"HAIL THE DAY THAT SEES HIM RISE," VERSE 1

Reflection: Three different meanings of the ascension of Christ are presented by today's Scripture texts. The passage from the Acts of the Apostles presumes a three-storied universe: heaven above, earth in the middle, the underworld below. The Jesus who came from heaven to earth now, forty days after his resurrection, returns to the heaven. This is echoed in verse one of "Hail the Day That Sees Him Rise" when the words state he returns to his throne above the skies on this day that sees him rise. The forty day period between Christ's resurrection and ascension is unique to the Acts of the Apostles.

In Luke's Gospel, written as volume one and Acts as volume two by the same author, the ascension occurs on Easter Sunday. After explaining to his disciples that it was necessary that he suffer and be raised from the dead on the third day, Jesus commissions them to preach repentance for the forgiveness of sins in his name. Then, he promises that they will be clothed with power from on high, a reference to the pyrotechnics accompanying the descent of the Holy Spirit in the Acts of the Apostles. Jesus leads them to Bethany, raises his hands, blesses them, and is taken to heaven. In other words, the major narrator of the ascension in the New Testament not only assigns it to two different days, but gives it two different meanings. In the gospel, Jesus must ascend in order for the Holy Spirit to descend a few days later.

The first option of a text from the Letter to the Ephesians is the same as in the Cycle A and Cycle B sets of Scripture texts; it depicts the enthronement of Christ at God's right hand. The second option, however, presents a passage from the Letter to the Hebrews. The author of Hebrews presumes that there is a carbon copy in heaven of what happens on earth. Just as the high priest enters the holy of holies once every year on earth, Jesus has entered the sanctuary in heaven once for all. There, he pleads before God on our behalf. His entry into the heavenly temple as the new high priest with his own blood gives us hope that one day we will follow him. So, according to Hebrews, Christ's ascension becomes our hope for entrance into heaven.

Meditation
Which meaning of the ascension gets most of your attention?
How can you apply that to your new life in Christ?

Prayer
Heavenly Father, you made your Son a great high priest through his offering of himself on the altar of the cross and taking away the sins of the world. Through his ascension to your right hand, you give hope to your pilgrim people. Grant that one day we may enter into the sanctuary where you live and reign with our Lord Jesus Christ and the Holy Spirit, one God, forever and ever. Amen.

Seventh Week of Easter

Monday of the Seventh Week of Easter

Scriptures
Acts 19:1–8;
John 16:29–33

Hymn
There for him high triumph waits; Alleluia!
Lift your heads eternal gates; Alleluia!
He has conquered death and sin; Alleluia!
Take the King of glory in. Alleluia!

"HAIL THE DAY THAT SEES HIM RISE," VERSE 2

Reflection: The second verse of "Hail the Day That Sees Him Rise" echoes the last line of today's gospel passage. In his farewell discourse in John's Gospel, Jesus tells his disciples to take courage because he has conquered the world. The verse of the hymn, echoing Psalm 24:7, 9, exhorts the gates of heaven to swing open to welcome the king of glory who conquered death and sin through his resurrection and ascension. However, while the application of the Psalm verses and the hymn verse are appropriate, Jesus has in mind a different kind of conquering. For the Johannine Jesus, conquering the world means convincing people that he came from God.

As he makes clear to his disciples, such belief is wonderful until it is attacked and the disciples flee to their homes. As long as no price is attached to faith, as long as it costs nothing, it is, indeed, wonderful! From reading the story many times, we know that they do flee when Jesus is arrested and crucified. We do the same. Someone asks us about a specific article of faith, and either we don't know the answer or we end up agreeing that such a position is weak rationally, biblically, or philosophically. We see the neighbors mowing the yard on Sunday and decide that such work is acceptable on the Lord's Day. We do not display religious items—like crosses, icons, statutes—in our homes because they may give our guests the wrong impression about us.

If we believe that Jesus, the king of glory, has conquered death and sin through his own death, resurrection, and ascension, then, like Paul in the passage from the Acts of the Apostles, we must continue to grow in faith. After Paul found twelve disciples in Ephesus and finds out that they received the baptism of John, he instructs them about the Holy Spirit, baptizes them in the name of Jesus, and, after laying his hands on their heads, gives them the gift of the Holy Spirit. They receive the gift and immediately put it to use bearing witness to the faith that Jesus died and God raised him to new life.

Meditation
In what specific ways do you herald Jesus as conqueror of death and sin?

Prayer
Heavenly Father, your only-begotten Son was put to death in order to conquer death. After your raised him to new life, he ascended to heaven and entered triumphantly through the gates of your kingdom and sent the Holy Spirit to those who believe in him. Give us the courage to bear witness to his name; he lives and reigns with you and the Holy Spirit as the king of glory forever and ever. Amen.

Tuesday of the Seventh Week of Easter

Scriptures
Acts 20:17–27;
John 17:1–11a

Hymn
Alleluia! sing to Jesus!
His the scepter, his the throne;
Alleluia! his the triumph,
His the victory alone:
Hark! The songs of peaceful Zion
Thunder like a mighty flood;
Jesus out of ev'ry nation
Has redeemed us by his blood.

Seventh Week of Easter

"ALLELUIA! SING TO JESUS!" VERSE 1

Reflection: The gospel passage for today, tomorrow, and Thursday is a continuous reading of chapter seventeen of John's Gospel. Chapter seventeen is Jesus' prayer to his Father. In today's first eleven verses of the prayer, the Johannine Jesus declares that his hour has come. The word "hour" has been used repeatedly throughout the Fourth Gospel to indicate Jesus' death and resurrection. Before this point, the phrase has been that his hour had not yet come. Now, before he is arrested and crucified, he asks the Father to glorify him so that he can glorify the Father through his death and resurrection. The brilliant holiness of God is revealed through the event of Jesus' death and resurrection. If this seems oxymoronic, it is meant to be so. The first verse of "Alleluia! Sing to Jesus!" captures this when we sing that Jesus has redeemed us by his blood. In other words, it is through his death and resurrection that he triumphs over death.

Jesus also prays to the Father for his disciples asking that through him they may receive eternal life, which is knowing the one true God and himself, Jesus Christ. He reminds God that he has revealed the Father's name to his followers; to reveal the name to them is to give them power to call upon God. He has also shared everything with them that the Father has shared with him so that they understand that he came from God and that he is getting ready to return to God. In other words, the one who came down from heaven and was made man is getting ready to die and return to heaven. He leaves behind those who have followed him and come to believe that he is the Son of God.

What awaits those who believe that Jesus is the Son of God is partially covered by Paul's farewell speech to the leaders of the church in Ephesus in the passage from the Acts of the Apostles. The apostle declares that he has been prompted by the Holy Spirit to head toward Jerusalem, where imprisonment and hardship await him. He will not hear the songs of peaceful Zion thundering like a mighty flood, but, nevertheless, he must finish his course, the ministry that the Lord Jesus entrusted to him. Paul refers to this as bearing witness to the gospel of God's grace. This means that Paul testifies to others the good news that God has poured himself on people through the death and resurrection of his Son, Jesus Christ. Paul expects to share in Jesus' suffering and death through his own in the hope of also sharing in the resurrection.

Overcome with Paschal Joy

Meditation

What hope do you find in Jesus' suffering, death, and resurrection? How is that hope nourished by Jesus' words in John's Gospel and Paul's words in the Acts of the Apostles?

Prayer

Father, you glorified your Son, Jesus Christ, through his death, resurrection, and ascension, and you poured the grace of the Holy Spirit on those who believed in him. Keep us attentive to the promptings of the Holy Spirit that we may do your will and come to share in eternal life. We ask this in the name of him who owns the victory, Jesus Christ, Lord and king forever and ever. Amen.

Wednesday of the Seventh Week of Easter

Scriptures
Acts 20:29–38;
John 17:11b–19

Hymn
Crown him, the Lord of peace,
Whose pow'r a scepter sways
From pole to pole, that wars may cease
Absorbed in prayer and praise:
His reign shall know no end,
And round his pierced feet
Fair flow'rs of paradise extend
Their fragrance ever sweet.

"CROWN HIM WITH MANY CROWNS," VERSE 3

Reflection: The passage from John's Gospel continues the twenty-six verse prayer of Jesus in chapter seventeen. In today's selection, Jesus prays for unity among his disciples as modeled by the unity between Jesus and the Father. If all are one, then they share in divine joy. Verse three of "Crown

Him with Many Crowns" echoes this sentiment when, after naming Jesus as Lord of peace, it states that under his kingship wars from one pole of the earth to the other will cease. People will be absorbed in prayer and praise. This ideal, announced in Jesus' prayer, has never been realized, of course.

In fact, over the past two thousand years the divisions within Christianity have often precipitated wars because disciples forget that they do not belong to this world, according to the Johannine Jesus. The world, which in John's Gospel is the adversary of heaven, hates the Father's word of peace. But because disciples remain in the world, even though they do not belong to it, Jesus prays that they be kept safe from its evil. Hopefully, they will learn from the example of Jesus, who himself did not belong to the world, how to be sent into it in order to draw others out of it to the Father. The complete joy that all can share in the Father's presence is characterized in the verse of today's hymn as paradisiacal flowers wafting sweet fragrances.

In the conclusion of his farewell speech to the leaders of the church of Ephesus in the passage from the Acts of the Apostles, Paul, too, is focused on the unity of the whole flock. Employing the image of sheep and shepherds, Paul tells the shepherds that evil, identified as savage wolves, will come and not spare the sheep by perverting the truth that Paul has shared with them for three years. As a result, disciples will be drawn away from the truth in which they have been consecrated or initiated. The Christian ideal—being in the world but not belonging to it—that both Jesus and Paul speak about remains today.

Meditation

How are you in the world but not of the world?
In other words, how do you live on the earth with your sights set on heaven?

Prayer

Holy Father, your Son prayed that all may be one as you and he are one. While we have not yet achieved that ideal, we pray that you will protect all people who continue to strive toward this goal. Grant that absorbed in prayer and praise we may remain consecrated in truth. We ask this through the Lord of peace, Jesus Christ, who lives and reigns with you and the Holy Spirit, one God, forever and ever. Amen.

Overcome with Paschal Joy

Thursday of the Seventh Week of Easter

Scriptures
Acts 22:30; 23:6–11;
John 17:20-26

Hymn
O grant that we through thee may come
To know the Father and the Son,
And hold with firm, unchanging faith,
That thou art Spirit of them both,
That thou art Spirit of them both.

"COME, HOLY GHOST, CREATOR BLEST," VERSE 4

Reflection: The Scripture passages presented on this last Thursday in the Easter Season represent the opposite ends of a continuum; one end is division, and the other end is unity. First, the passage from the Acts of the Apostles represents the division that occurs because of Paul's preaching in the Jewish community composed of Sadducees and Pharisees. Sadducees, the priestly aristocracy of Paul's time, did not believe in any type of resurrection, while the Pharisees, the teachers of the Law of Paul's time, did believe in some type or resurrection. Since Paul was a Pharisee, that party sided with him. This causes a division within Judaism, and Paul has to be rescued from the gathering.

Second, in the concluding section of his lengthy prayer in John's Gospel, Jesus extends his request for unity from him and his disciples to that of all who will believe in him through the disciples' preaching. In other words, Jesus petitions the Father to make all one, as the Father is in Jesus and Jesus is in the Father, that all may be one in them and brought to perfection as one. Then, he states that he has loved his disciples with the same love that he and the Father love each other in order to make Father, Son, and disciples one.

Most people find themselves standing somewhere on the continuum between the two extremes of division and unity. While we may gaze hopefully toward unity, we look over our shoulder to see lots of division in the

Christian church. The fourth verse of "Come, Holy Ghost, Creator Blest" is a prayer to the Holy Spirit, asking that the pray-er may come to know the Father and the Son and to know that the Spirit is the Spirit of them both. When the Nicene Creed (Profession of Faith) is recited, we say that we believe in the Holy Spirit, who proceeds from the Father and the Son. Thus, while our prayer is one for unity, we cannot pretend that the path to it is not paved with divisions that continue to draw our attention away from it.

Meditation

Where you do find yourself on the continuum between division and unity? How has your place on the continuum been influenced by your experiences of division or unity?

Prayer

Come, Holy Spirit, and reveal the Father and the Son to us. Come, and heal the source of our division that we may hold with firm, unchanging faith the unity of the Godhead: Father, Son, and Holy Spirit forever and ever. Amen.

Friday of the Seventh Week of Easter

Scriptures

Acts 25:13b–21;
John 21:15–19

Hymn

Where streams of living water flow
With gentle care he leads me,
And where the verdant pastures grow
With heav'nly food he feeds me.

"THE KING OF LOVE MY SHEPHERD IS," VERSE 2

Reflection: In the passage from what is known as the appendix or epilogue to John's Gospel, that is, a chapter added on after the rest of the text was

Overcome with Paschal Joy

written, Jesus has revealed himself as risen from the dead to seven of his disciples and fed them a heavenly breakfast on the shore of the living-water lake in which they had been fishing. Today's passage serves as the rehabilitation of Peter, who had three times denied knowing Jesus and now three times professes his love for Jesus. As Jesus asks Peter if he loves him and Peter declares that he does, Jesus commissions him to feed his lambs and his sheep, that is, all those who will come to believe in him through Peter's ministry. The passage ends with an echo of Jesus' call to Peter to follow him.

The passage from the Acts of the Apostles explains how Paul ultimately got to Rome according to the Acts of the Apostles. Felix, Roman governor of Judea, was succeeded by Festus, whom King Herod Agrippa II and Bernice, his wife, visited. When Felix left Caesarea, he also left Paul in prison there. Festus tells Herod Agrippa II that when he took over the governorship, he heard Paul's case and discovered that he was not guilty of any crimes. Rather, the Jews were upset with him because he kept talking about Jesus, who had died and been raised to life. Festus tells Herod that he wanted Paul to go to Jerusalem and stand trial, but Paul appealed his case to the emperor. Thus, Paul was held in custody until he could be sent to Rome, where Caesar (Nero) would decide his fate.

Both biblical passages illustrate how God cares for his people and directs their ways according to his will. Simon Peter is rehabilitated as one of the leaders of the early church. While it is not found in the Bible, tradition holds that Peter made his way to Rome, where he was martyred sometime in the sixth decade of the first century CE. Paul, too, made it to Rome, where he was martyred around the same time. These two men, Peter and Paul, are the twin heroes of the Acts of the Apostles. Whatever Jesus does in Luke's Gospel, Peter and Paul do in the Acts: heal a cripple, raise a dead person, eat meals, pray, etc. God's gentle care led them to the verdant pastures of Rome, from where they grew a church.

Meditation
Where has God's gentle care led you?
What did you grow?

Prayer
Gentle Father, you never leave your flock unguarded, but supply the church with leaders like Peter and Paul. Send us good ministers who guide us to the

streams of the living water of your grace that enable us to produce much fruit. Make us grateful for the heavenly food you provide, the body and blood of your Son, Jesus Christ, who lives and reigns with you and the Holy Spirit, one God, forever and ever. Amen.

Saturday of the Seventh Week of Easter

Scriptures
Acts 28:16–20, 30–31;
John 21:20–25

Hymn
Holy Father, Holy Son, Holy Spirit,
Three we name thee;
While in essence only One,
Undivided God we claim thee;
And adoring bend the knee,
While we own the mystery.

"HOLY GOD, WE PRAISE THY NAME," VERSE 4

Reflection: The fourth verse of "Holy God, We Praise Thy Name," expresses the doctrine of the Most Holy Trinity. There are three persons—Father, Son, Spirit—in one essence, one undivided God. Before such a mystery all people can do is adore on bended knee. And on this second to last day of the Easter Season, that is a good position to assume.

The Scripture texts offered to us on this Saturday of the Seventh Week of Easter contain their own mysteries. A mystery is an event or something that is difficult to understand. The passage from the end of the Acts of the Apostles explains how Paul got to Rome, lived alone under the guard of one Roman soldier, and continued to preach the kingdom of God and the Lord Jesus Christ to Jews and Gentiles while under house arrest for two years. The author of the Acts does not narrate Paul's death—traditionally understood as beheading—in the sixth decade of the first century. In iconography, Paul is usually depicted holding a sword to indicate the way he

Overcome with Paschal Joy

died. The mystery of this account in Acts is why the author, who wrote around thirty years after Paul's death, does not narrate that part of the story.

There is also mystery surrounding the additional chapter appended to John's Gospel. It can be clearly seen that the Fourth Gospel ends with 20:30–31. However, another author added chapter twenty-one, often labeled an epilogue or appendix in most Bibles. Today's passage comes from the end of the epilogue and features the unnamed beloved disciple, who makes his first appearance in John's Gospel during the supper (cf. 13:23). He appears again at the cross with Jesus' unnamed mother (cf. 19:26) and with Peter when Mary Magdalene announces the empty tomb (cf. 20:2). Thus, like other characters in John's Gospel—Nicodemus, Thomas, etc.—he appears three times, except he makes two more in the additional chapter (cf. 21:7, 20) and thus interrupts the structural scheme. In an effort to give him a name, many people refer to him as John, even though there is no internal evidence for such identification. Thus, he remains a mystery.

Meditation
What is one mystery of God's presence or work in your life?

Prayer
Holy Father, Holy Son, Holy Spirit, we name you, Almighty God. While in essence only one, undivided, we adore you and praise you. Give us the courage of Paul and the strength of the beloved disciple to share the mystery of your Godhead. We ask this through our Lord Jesus Christ, who lives and reigns with you, Father, and the Holy Spirit, one God, forever and ever. Amen.

15

Solemnity of Pentecost

Solemnity of the Vigil of Pentecost

Scriptures
Genesis 11:1–9;
Exodus 19:3–8a, 16–20b;
Ezekiel 37:1–14; Joel 3:1–5;
Romans 8:22–27;
John 7:37–39

Hymn
Now let us praise Father and Son
And Holy Spirit, with them one;
And may the Son on us bestow
The gifts that from the Spirit flow,
The gifts that from the Spirit flow.

"COME, HOLY GHOST, CREATOR BLEST," VERSE 5

Reflection: The Solemnity of Pentecost begins at 4 p.m. on the Saturday before Pentecost Sunday, which in the whole liturgical year ranks after the Paschal Triduum (Holy Thursday, Good Friday, Easter Sunday), the Nativity of the Lord (Christmas), the Epiphany, and the Ascension. Thus, because of its importance, like Easter it has its own vigil, and its Scripture texts illustrate a variety of images that help us understand the gift of the Holy Spirit.

Pentecost undoes the confusion of tongues at the tower of Babel in the Book of Genesis; after the Spirit descends on the apostles, people are able to understand each other's language. The Spirit comes with the same pyrotechnics that accompany the story of Moses' encounter with God on Mount Sinai in the Book of Exodus: thunder, lightning, cloud, smoke, fire, and earthquake. The Spirit comes from the four winds and breathes life into dry human bones in Ezekiel's vision, causing God to promise to open the graves of his people and raise them, just like he opened the tomb of Jesus and breathed new life into him. Through the prophet Joel, God promises to pour his Spirit upon all flesh which is exactly what happens on the day of Pentecost.

According to Paul in his Letter to the Romans, it is the Spirit who interprets the groanings we make in prayer and presents them to God. And according to Jesus in John's Gospel, he is the fountain from which anyone can drink the living water of the Spirit. A modern image might help us to understand that we are immersed in the Holy Spirit. Imagine a swimming pool full of water (Spirit) and full of swimmers. Under the water we can hear the talking and splashing of those around us because the water carries the sound to our ears. Furthermore, all in the pool are connected through the same water than envelopes them and gives them life. When swimmers emerge from the pool, they are refreshed and ready to face whatever comes next in their day. In the Holy Spirit we live and move and have our being; in the Holy Spirit we are guided, refreshed, and breathe eternal life.

Meditation
What is your favorite image of the Holy Spirit?

Prayer
We praise you, Father, Son, and Holy Spirit. We praise you, Father, for creating the world and all that is in it. We praise you, Jesus Christ, the Father's Son, for redeeming the world and all that is in it through your death and resurrection. We praise you, Holy Spirit, for breathing new life into the world re-created by God through Christ. All glory be to you, Holy Trinity, forever and ever. Amen.

Solemnity of Pentecost

Solemnity of Pentecost, Cycle A

Scriptures
Acts 2:1–11;
1 Corinthians 12:3b–7, 12–13;
John 20:19–23

Hymn
Come, Holy Ghost, Creator blest,
And in our hearts take up thy rest;
Come with thy grace and heav'nly aid
To fill the hearts which thou hast made,
To fill the hearts which thou hast made.

"COME, HOLY GHOST, CREATOR BLEST," VERSE 1

Reflection: Verse one of "Come, Holy Ghost, Creator Blest" adequately summarizes today's Scripture texts. The passage from the Acts of the Apostles declares that the strong driving wind of Pentecost fills the entire house in which the apostles are staying and fills them with the Holy Spirit. This results in immediate abilities, such as speaking in different tongues about the mighty acts of God. In the edited passage from Paul's First Letter to the Corinthians, the apostle focuses on the unity engendered in the community of believers by the Holy Spirit. While there are different spiritual gifts, different forms of service, and different workings among the community members, there is one Holy Spirit producing unity out of diversity. According to Paul, the individual manifestation of the Holy Spirit in terms of a person's particular gift is for the benefit of the whole community.

While Pentecost occurs fifty days after Easter in the Acts of the Apostles, Pentecost occurs on Easter Sunday evening in John's Gospel. The disciples are hiding behind locked doors when Jesus comes and stands among them. He breathes on them, telling them to receive the Holy Spirit. Then, he sends them into the world, like his Father had send him into the world, and he commissions them to forgive sins. The word in Greek for Spirit is the same word for breath and wind. So, Jesus blows open the locked doors of the place where the disciples are gathered and the locked doors of their

Overcome with Paschal Joy

hearts. The Holy Spirit takes residence within them, filling them with grace and being the aid Jesus promised them before his death and resurrection. The result is a unity of mission.

In a culture that focuses on the individual and the exploitation of his or her gifts to make lots of money in an extreme manner, the celebration of Pentecost with its emphasis on the unity of the community and the use of the individual members' gifts to benefit all serves as an antidote. When we sing, "Come, Holy Ghost, Creator Blest," we are asking the Holy Spirit to re-create us into one body with many parts. It was into the one Spirit that we were baptized into the one body and given to drink of the one Spirit. It makes no difference who we are or what we do. What matters is that we let the Spirit create unity out of our diversity.

Meditation
How have you used the gifts of the Holy Spirit given to you
for the common good? What unity has the Spirit realized through you?

Prayer
Come, Holy Spirit, and shed a ray of divine fire upon your people. Come, Holy Spirit, and fill us with your grace. Come, Holy Spirit, and take up your rest in our hearts. Out of our individual gifts craft the one body of Christ, who lives and reigns with you and the Father, one God, forever and ever. Amen.

Solemnity of Pentecost, Cycle B

Scriptures
Acts 2:1–11;
1 Corinthians 12:3b–7, 12–13 or Galatians 5:16–25;
John 20:19–23 or 15:26–27, 16:12–15

Hymn
O Comforter, to thee we cry,
Thou heav'nly gift of God most high,
Thou font of life and fire of love,
And sweet anointing from above,

Solemnity of Pentecost

And sweet anointing from above.
"COME HOLY GHOST, CREATOR BLEST," VERSE 2

Reflection: While the same biblical texts can be used in all three Sunday cycles for the Solemnity of Pentecost, in Cycle B two optional texts are presented. The first Scripture text is always the account of Pentecost found at the beginning of chapter two in the Acts of the Apostles. In Cycle B, the alternate text from Paul's Letter to the Galatians pits Spirit and flesh against each other. Paul understands the Spirit to be the Spirit of God who raised Jesus from the dead and breathed new life into him. The flesh is self-indulgence. Those who live in the Spirit manifest their way of life by love, joy, peace, patience, kindness, generosity, faithfulness, gentleness, and self-control. Those who live in the flesh manifest their way of life by immorality, impurity, lust, idolatry, sorcery, hatreds, rivalry, jealousy, outbursts of fury, acts of selfishness, dissensions, factions, occasions of envy, drinking bouts, and orgies. In other words, a person's lifestyle illustrates whether he or she is living in the Spirit or living in the flesh.

In the alternate text from John's Gospel, a small section of Jesus' farewell discourse to his disciples, Jesus names the Holy Spirit as the Advocate, also translated from Greek as Paraclete or Comforter, as in verse two of "Come Holy Ghost, Creator Blest." The Holy Spirit is an intercessor with God, much like a lawyer is a person's intercessor with a judge and jury. The Holy Spirit is a spokesperson, a mediator, a gift from God, the font of life, the fire of love. No one understanding adequately captures the meaning of the Spirit of truth in John's Gospel.

Thus, there is an ambiguity about the Holy Spirit presented on Pentecost Sunday. The author of the Scriptures cannot accurately describe who the Holy Spirit is. The images used—wind, fire, tongues, lifestyle manifestations, Advocate, truth—simultaneously tell us something about the Holy Spirit, but they also tell us nothing! The image is just that: an image. The image is not the Holy Spirit, who is like a sweet anointing from above.

Meditation
What image used for the Holy Spirit gets most of your attention?
What does the image disclose to you about the Spirit?

Overcome with Paschal Joy

What does the image hide about the Spirit?

Prayer

Holy Spirit, Comforter, gift of the Father, we cry to you: As the font of new life, give us to drink; as the fire of love, move us to generosity; and as sweet anointing, fill us with the courage to declare that Jesus is Lord forever and ever. Amen.

Solemnity of Pentecost, Cycle C

Scriptures

Acts 2:1–11;
1 Corinthians 12:3b–7, 12–13 or Romans 8:8–17;
John 20:19–23 or 14: 15–16, 23b–26

Hymn

To ev'ry sense thy light part, part
And shed thy love in ev'ry heart.
To our weak flesh, thy strength supply:
Unfailing courage from on high,
Unfailing courage from on high.

"COME, HOLY GHOST, CREATOR BLEST," VERSE 3

Reflection: While the same biblical texts can be used in all three Sunday cycles for the Solemnity of Pentecost, in Cycle C two optional texts are presented. The first Scripture text is always the account of Pentecost found at the beginning of chapter two in the Acts of the Apostles. In Cycle C, the alternate text from Paul's Letter to the Romans presents the typical Pauline understanding of the opposition of Spirit and flesh. This is also found in the third verse of "Come, Holy Ghost, Creator Blest;" the singers ask the Holy Spirit to supply strength to their weak flesh so that they may have unfailing courage. However, Paul also states that if the Spirit of God, who raised Jesus from the dead, dwells in people, then God, who raised Christ from the dead, will give life to mortal bodies through his Spirit dwelling in them. Then, the apostle emphasizes that those who are led by God's Spirit are God's adopted children. If they are God's adopted children, then they are joint heirs with Christ, whose body they form. And they are promised glorification, resurrection from the dead, just like Jesus received.

In the alternate, pieced-together passage from some of the verses forming Jesus' farewell discourse in John's Gospel, Jesus promises those who love him another Advocate. The reader must keep in mind that Jesus is the first advocate; the other Advocate, identified as the Holy Spirit, whom the Father sends in Jesus' name, will serve as the disciples' new teacher. Jesus, the incarnate word of God, is impermanent; he is getting ready to leave. The Holy Spirit will be a permanent teacher. While the emphasis is on continued education for the disciples, the passage revolves on love, mentioned four times.

The love that is at the core of John's Gospel and that verse three of the hymn asks be shed in every heart comes from the Holy Spirit. In John's Gospel, that is referred to as self-sacrificing love. It means that a person always puts others ahead of himself or herself in imitation of Jesus. More importantly, a person puts the love of Jesus above all else. Human self-sacrificing love enables the keeping of divine commandments and paves the way for receiving the Father's love, named the Holy Spirit. Verse three of the hymn asks that the Holy Spirit imparts his light to every human sense. Thus, the total human person is educated by the Holy Spirit until the day of death and glorification.

Meditation
What has the Holy Spirit taught you about love?

Prayer
Come, Holy Spirit, and impart to every sense your divine light. Come, Holy Spirit, and shed your love in every heart. Come, Holy Spirit, and fill us with unfailing courage to proclaim that God is our Father, that Jesus is our brother, and that you are our teacher. All praise be to you, eternal Trinity, forever and ever. Amen.

16

Feasts and Solemnities

During Lent and Easter, there are several feasts and solemnities that are celebrated in place of the Lenten or Easter weekday. They are listed below. Each has directions indicating when it is marked or omitted.

February 22: Feast of the Chair of St. Peter the Apostle

When this feast falls on a weekday during Lent, it takes precedence over the Lenten weekday. If it falls on a Sunday, it is omitted.

Scriptures
1 Peter 5:1-4;
Matthew 16:13–19

Hymn
And so through all the length of days
Your goodness fails me never;
Good Shepherd, may I sing your praise
Within your house for ever.

"THE KING OF LOVE MY SHEPHERD IS," VERSE 6

Reflection: The word "chair" in the title of this feast does not refer to a physical seat with a back support—maybe armrests—and having four legs.

Rather, "chair" refers to a position of ministry that is usually attributed to the pope, the successor of Peter, as today's Scripture texts attest. The passage from the First Letter of St. Peter is an exhortation to leaders to tend the flock of God as God would. This means that the leader must give good example to the sheep until the chief shepherd, Jesus, returns in glory. In Christian tradition, the attribute of shepherd, given to the LORD in Psalm 23, is applied to Jesus in First Peter. Thus, today's Responsorial Psalm 23 points back to the Hebrew Bible (Old Testament) concept of God as shepherd and forward to the Christian Bible (New Testament) concept of Jesus as the good shepherd.

The passage from Matthew's Gospel is one that is chosen to be read on many celebrations having to do with St. Peter or the pope or both. Found first in Mark's Gospel, the author of Matthew's Gospel rewrites the story of Jesus traveling in the region of Caesarea Philippi and asking his disciples about who people are saying he is. Peter, who occupies a much loftier place in Matthew's Gospel than he does in Mark's, declares that Jesus is the anointed (Christ), the Son of the living God. This means that Peter is stating that Jesus is the Messiah (anointed), God's chosen one. Jesus praises Peter's ability to discern this.

Then, in a passage unique to Matthew's Gospel, Jesus declares Peter to be the rock upon which he will build his church. It is important for the reader to know that "petrus" is the Greek word for "rock" and from which comes the name "Peter." This is a play on words. Then, the Matthean Jesus tells Peter that he gives him the keys to the kingdom of heaven; later in the narrative, Jesus will give the keys to the kingdom of heaven to everyone, but this is not our interest here. The focus here is on the authority of Peter to bind and to lose. For two thousand years those who have succeeded Peter and been called pope from the twelfth century have claimed this authority which is represented by a chair. Thus, today's feast honors the authority of Peter and his successors through the length of days.

Meditation

What significance do you find in honoring the authority of Peter and his successors in the church using the image of a chair?

Overcome with Paschal Joy

Prayer

You are our shepherd, O LORD, leading us to verdant pastures and beside restful waters. Be with us when we walk through the dark valleys of life so that only goodness and kindness follow us through the length of our days. Bring us one day to your house, where you live and reign with our Lord Jesus Christ, the Good Shepherd, and the Holy Spirit, one God, forever and ever. Amen.

March 19: Solemnity of St. Joseph, Spouse of the Blessed Virgin Mary

When this solemnity falls on a weekday during Lent, it takes precedence over the Lenten weekday. When this solemnity falls on a weekday during the Easter Season, it takes precedence over the Easter weekday. If it falls on a Sunday during Lent or Easter, it is celebrated on the following Monday, unless that Monday is Monday of Holy Week or Monday of the First Week of Easter. When this solemnity falls during Holy Week or Easter Week, it is celebrated on Monday of the Second Week of Easter.

Scriptures
2 Samuel 7:4–5a, 12–14a, 16;
Romans 4:13, 16–18, 22;
Matthew 1:16, 18–21, 24a or Luke 2:41–51a

Hymn
Songs of thankfulness and praise,
Jesus, Lord, to thee we raise;
Manifested by the star
To the sages from afar,
Branch of royal David's stem
In thy birth at Bethlehem:
Anthems be to thee addressed,
God in flesh made manifest.

"SONGS OF THANKFULNESS AND PRAISE," VERSE 1

Feasts and Solemnities

Reflection: At first it might seem odd that verse one of "Songs of Thankfulness and Praise" about Jesus—and a hymn associated with his Epiphany and Baptism—be used for the Solemnity of the St. Joseph, Spouse of the Blessed Virgin Mary. However, upon careful examination, the reader will find that this verse summarizes the biblical texts assigned to this feast. It is Matthew's Gospel that identifies Joseph as a son of David through a complicated spiritual (not historical) genealogy. This status is further emphasized by the passage from the Second Book of Samuel in which the LORD speaks to his prophet Nathan and sends him to King David with the promise that God will make his royal throne, house, and kingdom secure forever. Historically, we know that David's line came to an end with King Zedekiah in 587 BCE. That is why Matthew's genealogy ending with Joseph is a spiritual one, as is the title "Son of David" applied to Jesus.

The Matthean Joseph is not only of the spiritual line of David, he is also a righteous man, that is, one who does the right thing because it is the right thing to do. In Matthew's Gospel, Joseph is the first model of righteousness, a theme that the author has woven throughout the work. When according to the Torah Joseph should have had Mary stoned because she was pregnant outside of marriage, the Matthean Joseph breaks Torah and takes her as his wife into his home. Sometimes in order to do the right thing, one may have to break the Law! St. Paul also addresses the concept of righteousness in his letter to the Romans. Paul praises the righteousness that comes from faith, whose best example is Abraham. The patriarch did the right thing, trusting God and hoping against hope when he had no son but God promised him that he would be the father of many nations. Abraham did the right thing again when God asked him to sacrifice his son, Isaac, and Abraham was willing to do so. Righteousness, according to Paul, is a gift that God offers to people; those who accept it, like Abraham and Joseph, are in a healthy relationship with God even though it may not look that way to Torah-abiding others.

Because the child Jesus is conceived through the Holy Spirit, according to Matthew, it is clear that Joseph is Jesus' foster-father. Thus, he can only be spiritually connected to King David. In Luke's Gospel it is Jesus' greatness that fulfills God's promise to David, not any connection to the defunct royal line. And while Joseph is mentioned in Luke's Gospel, he is never given a line to speak, as can be seen in today's optional gospel passage. Furthermore, in Luke's Gospel, Joseph's father is named Heli, whereas it is Jacob in Matthew! Clearly, both evangelists consider their genealogies spiritual.

The focus of this solemnity, thus, is Jesus, who in Matthew's Gospel was manifested by a star to sages, who traveled to Bethlehem—where the author of Matthew's Gospel presumes Joseph and Mary live. Jesus' birth place is the same birth place as King David! Jesus is hailed as a spiritual branch of royal David's stem because of his foster-father, Joseph, and his birth place. Thus, Joseph's importance flows directly backward from Christ's importance.

Meditation
As you sort through all the above information on Joseph, what conclusion do you reach?

Prayer
We raise songs of thankfulness and praise to you, Lord Jesus, for revealing yourself as the incarnate God to your foster-father Joseph and to sages who followed your star to Bethlehem. As we honor Joseph this day, grant that we might respond in righteousness to your call. Hear the anthems we address to you and to your Father in the unity of the Holy Spirit, one God, forever and ever. Amen.

March 25: The Solemnity of the Annunciation of the Lord

When this solemnity falls on a weekday during Lent, it takes precedence over the Lenten weekday. When this solemnity falls on a weekday during the Easter Season, it takes precedence over the Easter weekday. If it falls on a Sunday during Lent or Easter, it is celebrated on the following Monday, unless that Monday is Monday of Holy Week or Monday of the First Week of Easter. When this solemnity falls during Holy Week or Easter Week, it is celebrated on Monday of the Second Week of Easter.

Scriptures
Isaiah 7:10–14, 8:10;
Hebrews 10:4–10;
Luke 1:26–38

Feasts and Solemnities

Hymn

Angels, from the realms of glory,
Wing your flight o'er all the earth;
Once you sang creation's story,
Now proclaim Messiah's birth:
Come and worship, come and worship,
Worship Christ, the newborn King.

"ANGELS, FROM THE REALMS OF GLORY," VERSE 1 AND REFRAIN

Reflection: The Solemnity of the Annunciation of the Lord is a biblical feast found only in Luke's Gospel. While Matthew's book contains an announcement to Joseph—one of the gospel options for the March 19 Solemnity of St. Joseph, Spouse of the Blessed Virgin Mary—the more familiar one concerns the (arch)angel Gabriel appearing to Mary in Nazareth and announcing that the Holy Spirit will come upon her and the power of the Most High God will overshadow her and she will conceive the Son of God. That annunciation is echoed in the passage from the prophet Isaiah, who records the LORD telling King Ahaz that one of the young women in his court will bear a son, who is to be named Emmanuel. Because he is in the midst of a war which he seems to be losing, this is good news for Ahaz. It becomes better news when the etymology of the name is revealed to the king: "God is with us!" In Christian tradition, this passage is understood as announcing the birth of Jesus. However, only the author of Matthew's Gospel quotes it in his announcement to Joseph.

The first verse and refrain from "Angels, from the Realms of Glory," echo today's gospel. Gabriel, from the realms of glory, that is, the world above where God lives, comes to the earth to proclaim that the Messiah will be born from the womb of Mary of Nazareth. The hymn declares that angels have wings, a difficult fact to prove since they are invisible! A winged person (bird-like and human) makes sense in a three-storied universe. The wings enable descent from and ascent to the heavens, while making the body recognizable on earth. One of the ways to join heaven and earth is with a winged person named Gabriel, whose name means "God's strength."

The passage from the Letter to the Hebrews adds another dimension to the aspect of annunciation. The unknown author of this text emphasizes that Christ came into the world to do God's will. Jesus did God's will by offering himself once for all. Likewise, Mary, his mother, did God's will by saying yes to Gabriel's message. Gabriel did God's will by delivering the Most High's request to the virgin. We, too, should consider those daily announcements that come from God through others, through the Bible, and maybe through angels requesting our participation in his will.

Meditation
What announcement have you most recently heard from God?
What did the Most High ask you to do? Did you do it?

Prayer
Most High God, you sent Gabriel to Mary to announce your plan to bring your Son into the world. Her willingness to do your will resulted in the birth of the Messiah. Send your Holy Spirit upon us that we may hear your word, conceive it in our heart, and do your will. We ask this through our Lord Jesus Christ, who lives and reigns with you, Father, and the Holy Spirit, one God, forever and ever. Amen.

April 25: Feast of St. Mark, Evangelist

When this feast falls on a weekday during the Easter Season, it takes precedence over the Easter weekday unless it falls during the First Week of Easter, when it is omitted. If it falls on a Sunday, it is omitted.

Scriptures
1 Peter 5:5b–14;
Mark 15:15–20

Hymn
Blessed feasts of blessed martyrs,
Holy women, holy men,
With our love and admiration,
Greet we your return again.
Worthy deeds they wrought and wonders,

Feasts and Solemnities

Worthy of the name they bore;
We with joyful praise and singing,
Honor them for evermore.

"BLESSED FEASTS OF BLESSED MARTYRS," VERSE 1

Reflection: Today's feast of the Evangelist Mark distinguishes him as a holy man, according to verse one of "Blessed Feasts of Blessed Martyrs." Mark, whoever he was, was not a martyr, but that does not mean that we cannot greet his annual feast day with our love and admiration, nor does it imply that we cannot sing joyful songs of honor for the one who wrote the oldest of the gospels around 70 CE: Mark. In many ways, writing the first and only book we name gospel (Matthew calls his work a book; Luke calls his an orderly account; and John has no name for his work), wrought a worthy deed by putting quill to papyrus sheets and leaving a narrative of the good news of the kingdom preached by Jesus.

The passage from the First Letter of Peter is presented only because it mentions the name "Mark" in the greetings to be relayed to those who read the work. Given the fact that Mark was a popular Latin name in the centuries when the Christian Bible (New Testament) was being written, this could be any of thousands of Marks. Even the "Gospel According to Mark" does not bear that name until the second century. So, an anonymous Mark must have written it or been associated with it somehow.

In a singular twist of irony, the passage from Mark's Gospel assigned for this feast comes from the third ending of the narrative. Yes, Mark's Gospel has three endings; most Bibles indicate that the original ending is 16:8; the shorter ending has two sentences added to 16:8; and the longer ending is 16:9–20, from which today's passage is extracted. This means that whoever wrote Mark's Gospel did not write the longer ending, which was composed by another author who did not like the original way the story ended!

Maybe it is better to focus on celebrating the gospel today than on the evangelist who wrote it. We are sent into the world with the good news that the kingdom of God is near. In his parables, Jesus compared it to ordinary agricultural events, like planting seed. In his speeches, Jesus attempted to awaken hearers to the kingdom's presence. And in his healings, Jesus enacted the power of the kingdom. As a good news announcer, that is, an evangelist, we are commissioned and sent with the same message.

Meditation
What is the good news of the kingdom of God
that you deliver through your words and deeds?

Prayer
O LORD, the heavens proclaim your wonders while those on earth proclaim your faithfulness. Grant that we who have heard the good news of your kingdom may proclaim it in word and deed. Keep us faithful to the message of your Son, Jesus Christ, who lives and reigns with you and the Holy Spirit, one God, forever and ever. Amen.

May 3: Feast of Sts. Philip and James, Apostles

When this feast falls on a weekday during the Easter Season, it takes precedence over the Easter weekday unless it falls during the First Week of Easter, when it is omitted. If it falls on a Sunday, it is omitted.

Scriptures
1 Corinthians 15:1–8;
John 14:6–14

Hymn
Holy, Holy, Holy! all the saints adore thee,
Casting down their golden crowns around the glassy sea;
Cherubim and seraphim falling down before thee,
God everlasting through eternity.
"HOLY, HOLY, HOLY!" VERSE 2

Feasts and Solemnities

Reflection: All the saints adore the everlasting God, according to verse two of "Holy, Holy, Holy!" Using imagery from the Book of Revelation, they cast their golden crowns around the sea of glass; the sea, representing chaos, has been turned into glassy order by God and the Lamb in the Book of Revelation. The two apostles honored today are among those twenty-four elders crying, "Holy, holy, holy!"

The first passage from Paul's First Letter to the Corinthians mentions that the apostle James was one of those who witnessed an appearance of the risen Christ. This James, not the brother of John, but who used to be known as James the Less (Junior), is also called the brother (cousin) of the Lord. In the Acts of the Apostles, he is known as James the Just and renders the decision after the meeting that decides that Gentiles who follow the Way do not need to be circumcised. He was most likely martyred in the sixth decade of the first century CE.

The passage from John's Gospel mentions the other apostle being honored today: Philip. This is not Philip in the Acts of the Apostles; that Philip is one of seven men chosen to wait on tables. This Philip is called by Jesus after he calls Andrew and Peter. In today's passage, Jesus seems to reprimand him for asking Jesus to show him the Father. Jesus asks him, "Have I been with you all this time, Philip, and you still do not know me?" (John 14:9) Then, Jesus makes clear that whoever has seen him has seen the Father.

This celebration of two among fifteen-plus apostles should prompt us to explore the meaning of the moniker. The word "apostle" means "sent." It can refer to an ambassador, delegate, or messenger. While the word has become almost exclusively associated with religious missionaries, its additional meanings of ambassador, delegate, or messenger can help explore the word's depth. Philip and James are ambassadors, that is, officials of the highest rank representing Jesus. They are delegates, that is, they have been given the authority to act on behalf of Jesus. And they are messengers, carrying good news from Jesus to others. All those meanings—and more—are contained in the moniker apostle.

Meditation
How are you an apostle?

Overcome with Paschal Joy

Prayer

Your glory, O God, is proclaimed by your creation of the heavens and the solar, lunar, and astral bodies that rise and set there. On earth the message of your Son is proclaimed by your apostles Philip and James. Send us with the good news preached by Jesus Christ, who lives and reigns with you and the Holy Spirit, one God, forever and ever. Amen.

May 14: Feast of St. Matthias, Apostle

When this feast falls on a weekday during the Easter Season, it takes precedence over the Easter weekday. If it falls on a Sunday, it is omitted.

Scriptures
Acts 1:15–17, 20–26;
John 15:9–17

Hymn
We would not live by bread alone,
But by your word of grace,
In strength of which we travel on
To our abiding place.

"SHEPHERD OF SOULS," VERSE 2

Reflection: St. Matthias is one of the apostles who makes a brief appearance in the Acts of the Apostles to be chosen as an apostle and then disappears, never to be written about again! We can only presume that the word of grace that called him to apostleship gave him enough strength to travel on to his abiding place with Christ. His story in the Acts begins with Peter's speech about Judas; today's passage is an edited version of Peter's narrative, leaving out the part about Judas' death in a field.

In order to have the full complement of apostles before Pentecost, a replacement must be elected to replace Judas. The basic requirement is having been a follower from Jesus' baptism by John the Baptist to his resurrection. Two candidates are proposed: Joseph called Barsabbas and known as Justus and Matthias. After praying with the one hundred twenty believers witnessing this event, Peter gave lots to them. This means that each was given a stone with his initial or mark on it, and the stones were placed in a container and shaken until one fell out. Matthias' stone came out first, and so he was added to the Eleven. And that is all we ever hear from or see of him again.

Because Matthias is elected in the Acts of the Apostles, his name does not appear in any gospel. The passage from John's Gospel is a part of Jesus' farewell discourse and represents a generic reflection on being chosen. The Johannine Jesus reminds his disciples that they did not choose him, but he chosen them. Then, he appointed them to go forth and bear fruit. Their being chosen and their bearing fruit is grounded in self-sacrificial love, the kind where one lays down his or her life for his or her friends in imitation of Jesus. Matthias' name captures this; it means "gift of God."

Meditation

When were you chosen by Jesus to be a disciple?
Does the meaning of your name shed any meaning on your discipleship?

Prayer

Almighty Father, your word of grace is a gift to your people, as is the apostle Matthias. Fill our hearts with the strength of self-sacrificing love that we may travel through this life bearing witness to you in the hope of finding an eternal abiding place, where you live and reign with your Son, our Lord Jesus Christ, in the unity of the Holy Spirit, forever and ever. Amen.

May 31: Feast of the Visitation of the Blessed Virgin Mary

When this feast falls on a weekday during the Easter Season, it takes precedence over the Easter weekday. If it falls on a Sunday, it is omitted.

Overcome with Paschal Joy

Scriptures
Zephaniah 3:14–18a or Romans 12:9–16;
Luke 1:39–56

Hymn
The Son you bore by heaven's grace, Alleluia:
Did all our guilt and sin efface, Alleluia,
Rejoice, rejoice, O Mary.

"BE JOYFUL, MARY, HEAV'NLY QUEEN," VERSE 2

Reflection: The Feast of the Visitation of the Blessed Virgin Mary is a biblical feast found only in Luke's Gospel. After the (arch)angel Gabriel tells Mary that her relative Elizabeth has conceived a child in her old age, Mary heads to the hill country where Zechariah and Elizabeth live; this is what is meant by her visitation. Upon entering the elderly couple's home, Elizabeth utters three beatitudes, calling Mary blessed among women, blessed for believing God's word, and blessing the fruit of her womb. The second verse of "Be Joyful, Mary, Heav'nly Queen," declares that Mary bore the Son by God's grace, and so she should rejoice. In response to Elizabeth's blessings, Mary sings a hymn.

The passage from the prophet Zephaniah echoes verse two of "Be Joyful, Mary, Heav'nly Queen" and Mary's hymn as it calls upon Jerusalem (Zion) to sing and to be glad in the hope that the kingdom of Judah, destroyed by the Babylonians in 587 BCE, will one day be restored. The hope for restoration is based on the LORD being named the King of Israel, instead of a Davidic heir. It is also founded on God being in the midst of his people, as is the case of Elizabeth greeting Mary, whose womb contains the Son of God.

The passage from Paul's letter to the Romans similarly emphasizes the rejoicing in hope provided by the prophet Zephaniah. Echoing Jesus' words about loving one's enemies, Paul tells the Romans to bless those who persecute them and not to curse them. They are to rejoice with those who rejoice. They are to love one another with mutual affection and to exercise hospitality, like that of Elizabeth, which anticipates the needs of others. As demonstrated by Elizabeth, biblical hospitality often entails serving God in one's midst.

Meditation

When you have shown hospitality to others and recognized the presence of God?

Prayer

Almighty God, holy is your name. You show mercy to those who show hospitality to others. We rejoice in your presence in word, sacrament, and people. Give us the ability to name your presence among us and to rejoice because you, the Holy One, are in our midst. You live and reign as Father, Son, and Holy Spirit forever and ever. Amen.

June 11: Memorial of St. Barnabas, Apostle

When this memorial falls on a weekday during the Easter Season, it takes precedence over the Easter weekday. If it falls on a Sunday, it is omitted.

Scriptures

Acts 11:21b–26; 13:1–3;
Matthew 10:7–13

Hymn

Lo! The apostolic train
Join the sacred Name to hallow;
Prophets swell the loud refrain,
And the white-robed martyrs follow;
And from morn to set of sun,
Through the Church the song goes on.

"HOLY GOD, WE PRAISE THY NAME," VERSE 3

Overcome with Paschal Joy

Reflection: Barnabas, a companion of Paul in the Acts of the Apostles, is a member of the apostolic train. He is introduced in chapter four of the Acts as a Levite, whose name was Joseph, but whom the apostles called Barnabas, meaning "son of encouragement." Later, Barnabas is sent by the apostles to Antioch to catechize believers there. The Acts identifies him as a good man, filled with the Holy Spirit and faith. Because of the work needing to be done, he goes to Tarsus, finds Saul (Paul), and brings him back to work for a year where the disciples were first called Christians. After a year, while at prayer, the Holy Spirit informs the gathering that Barnabas and Saul (Paul) are to be set apart for missionary work.

From chapter thirteen to chapter fifteen, Paul and Barnabas travel around the known world establishing Christian communities. However, near the end of chapter fifteen, they have a disagreement, and they part company. Barnabas joins with John Mark, and Paul joins with Silas. And except for mentions in Paul's First Letter to the Corinthians, his letter to the Galatians, and the letter to the Colossians that is all we know about Barnabas, who from sunrise to sunset preached about the death and resurrection of Jesus Christ.

The passage from Matthew's Gospel is a part of Jesus' missionary discourse in that book. The basic message is that God's kingdom is here. Just as Jesus has enacted its arrival, apostles are to cure the sick, raise the dead, cleans the lepers, and drive out demons. In other words, they have received the good news without cost; therefore, they are to give it to others without a charge. In a modern world fueled by consumerism, giving away anything without cost seems to be a foolish practice. It is in this cultural fact that the deep truth of the gospel shines. The church offers the good news to all without cost, and the song goes on.

Meditation
In what specific ways have you given the gospel to others without cost?

Prayer
LORD God, you have made known the salvation of your Son to all the nations of the world through the ministry of your apostle Barnabas. As we remember him who hallowed your sacred name, send us to proclaim the arrival of your kingdom. From morning to evening may you be praised in one unending

chorus, Father, with our Lord Jesus Christ in the unity of the Holy Spirit, forever and ever. Amen.

Seventh Sunday of Easter, Cycle A

When the Solemnity of the Ascension of the Lord is celebrated on Thursday of the Sixth Week of Easter, the Sunday between Ascension and the Solemnity of Pentecost is the Seventh Sunday of Easter. When Ascension is celebrated on the Sunday before Pentecost, the Seventh Sunday of Easter is omitted. However, the second reading and gospel from the Seventh Sunday of Easter may be used in place of those provided for the Sixth Sunday of Easter.

Scriptures
Acts 1:12–14;
1 Peter 4:13-16;
John 17:1–11a

Hymn
Faith of our fathers! faith and prayer
Shall win all nations unto thee;
And through the truth that comes from God,
Mankind shall then indeed be free.
Faith of our fathers, holy faith!
We will be true to thee till death.

"FAITH OF OUR FATHERS!" VERSE 3 AND REFRAIN

Reflection: The passage from the Acts of the Apostles read in the A Cycle of Scripture texts for the Seventh Sunday of Easter presumes that the Solemnity of the Ascension of the Lord has already been celebrated on the Thursday before. The opening line of the passage from the Acts mentions that Jesus has been taken to heaven. Then, it proceeds to mention the names of eleven apostles, some women, Mary the mother of Jesus, and his brothers devoted

Overcome with Paschal Joy

to prayer. Their prayer demonstrates the faith to which they will be true till death, as is mentioned in the verse in the above hymn. Their prayer will ultimately lead them to nominate two candidates and choose one to replace Judas so that the Twelve are reconstituted before Pentecost.

The third verse and refrain of "Faith of Our Fathers!" is also echoed in the passage from the First Letter of St. Peter. According to this document, there are two kinds of suffering. There is bad suffering which results from evil deeds, and there is good suffering which results from insults for proclaiming the name of Christ, of which one should not be ashamed. The author of this letter considers being insulted for the name of Christ a blessing.

The gospel passage is the same as that for Tuesday of the Seventh Week of Easter. Jesus announces that his hour has come; up to this point in the narrative the writer has repeatedly told the reader that his hour had not yet come. The word "hour" refers to his suffering, death, resurrection, and glorification. Set into the context of a prayer to the Father, Jesus prays for his disciples, asking the Father to protect those who believe in him and receive the truth that he has shared with them from God. They will remain in the world to continue to win the nations, but Jesus is preparing to leave the world.

Meditation
In your family who has preceded you in faith:
grandfathers, grandmothers, father, mother, etc.?
What did each contribute to the faith you now have?

Prayer
Father, our holy faith stands on the shoulders of your Son's apostles and countless men and women of the past who have believed and taught the truth that comes from you. Keep us full of faith that we may dwell in freedom in your house all the days of this life and enter into your eternal dwelling in the next. We ask this through our Lord Jesus Christ, your Son, who lives and reigns with you and the Holy Spirit, one God, forever and ever. Amen.

Feasts and Solemnities

Seventh Sunday of Easter, Cycle B

When the Solemnity of the Ascension of the Lord is celebrated on Thursday of the Sixth Week of Easter, the Sunday between Ascension and the Solemnity of Pentecost is the Seventh Sunday of Easter. When Ascension is celebrated on the Sunday before Pentecost, the Seventh Sunday of Easter is omitted. However, the second reading and gospel from the Seventh Sunday of Easter may be used in place of those provided for the Sixth Sunday of Easter.

Scriptures
Acts 1:15–17, 20a, 20c–26;
1 John 4:11–16;
John 17:11b–19

Hymn
Oh, blest communion! fellowship divine!
We feebly struggle, they in glory shine!
Yet all are one in thee, for all are thine!
Alleluia! Alleluia!

"FOR ALL THE SAINTS," VERSE 4

Reflection: The narrative concerning the election of Matthias to replace Judas as a member of the twelve apostles in the passage from the Acts of the Apostles is also read on the Feast of St. Matthias, May 14. After two candidates are presented—Judas (also called Barsabbas and known as Justus) and Matthias—lots fell to Matthias, and he was counted with the eleven apostles. In the words of verse four from "For All the Saints," Matthias enters into the blessed communion of apostleship and divine fellowship. The twelve are reconstituted as one body in preparation for Pentecost. After Matthias is elected, nothing is ever written about him or about Judas (also called Barsabbas and known as Justus) again. In other words, Matthias' sole purpose is to be apostle number twelve!

The blessed communion and divine fellowship is also the topic of the passage from the First Letter of St. John. Here, the basis is not election, but self-sacrificing love. The message is simple: God is love, and God loves us self-sacrificially, as demonstrated in his Son, Jesus Christ, who loved us to his death on the cross. Those who acknowledge that Jesus is God's Son and savior of the world have been given God's love. When they love one another, they simultaneously love God and Jesus. Thus, those who remain in love remain in God and God in them. Such self-sacrificing love puts others ahead of oneself, just like the unseen God's love was put ahead of himself in the incarnation of the seen Jesus.

The passage from John's Gospel is the same as that read on Wednesday of the Seventh Week of Easter. It is a part of Jesus' farewell discourse and prayer for his disciples, who will have to struggle in the world while he shines in glory. Jesus asks God to protect them; they cannot be taken out of the world, but the Holy Father can keep the evil one away from them. They are sent into the world, even though they do not belong to it. And so Jesus prays that they be one in him as he is one in God so that God may be one in them.

Meditation

In what specific ways do you experience communion or divine fellowship now? What struggles accompany it?

Prayer

Holy Father, from the beginning of creation you have desired that your people be one in the love that you share with your Son and the Holy Spirit. Keep all division from our lives as we struggle toward communion. Bring your divine love to perfection in us. Father, grant this through our Lord Jesus Christ, your Son, who lives in fellowship with the Holy Spirit, one God, forever and ever. Amen.

Seventh Sunday of Easter, Cycle C

When the Solemnity of the Ascension of the Lord is celebrated on Thursday of the Sixth Week of Easter, the Sunday between Ascension and the Solemnity of Pentecost is the Seventh Sunday of Easter. When Ascension is celebrated on the Sunday before Pentecost, the Seventh

Sunday of Easter is omitted. However, the second reading and gospel from the Seventh Sunday of Easter may be used in place of those provided for the Sixth Sunday of Easter.

Scriptures
Acts 7:55–60;
Revelation 22:12–14, 16–17, 20;
John 17:20–26

Hymn
For all the saints, who from their labors rest,
Who thee by faith before the world confessed,
Thy name, O Jesus, be for ever blessed. Alleluia! Alleluia!

"FOR ALL THE SAINTS," VERSE 1

Reflection: The passage from the Acts of the Apostles is a much shorter version of an already shortened edition of the death of Stephen presented on Tuesday of the Third Week of Easter. Stephen, one of seven men chosen to wait on tables by the apostles, is one of those saints mentioned in verse one of "For All the Saints" who now rests from his labors. Stephen's death is modeled after Jesus' death in Luke's Gospel. The final lines that both Jesus and Stephen say are almost identical. Thus, the one who confessed the name of Jesus before the world saw him standing at God's right hand in heaven and died like him, forgiving his enemies. The only difference is that Jesus was crucified while Stephen was stoned.

The passage from the end of the Book of Revelation portrays the heavenly Jesus informing John of Patmos that he is coming soon. In fact, the book ends with the petition, "Come, Lord Jesus!" (22:20) This prayer has never been realized; the hope for Jesus' return in glory is stated here and focused intently during the first two weeks of Advent in early December. We are still waiting in joyful hope for his coming. The Book of Revelation applies several monikers to his name that are worthy of reflection while waiting for his return. First, he is Alpha and Omega, the first and last letters of the Greek alphabet; he is the beginning and the end of all things.

Second, he is the spiritual root and offspring of David, as written about by the prophet Isaiah. Third, he is the bright morning star, that is, the sun, whose light dispels all darkness.

The passage from John's Gospel, which is the same as that on Thursday of the Seventh Week of Easter, concludes Jesus' farewell discourse. In this last section, Jesus prays to the Father for unity. The unity of believers is modeled on the unity shared by the Father and the Son. Jesus asks that his disciples may be one in the Father and the Son the way that God is in Jesus and Jesus is in the Father. Such unity will be a sign to others to believe that God sent Jesus and gave him the disciples as a gift. One day, they, the saints who have professed their faith, will rest from their labors in the place Jesus is preparing for them.

Meditation

Which of the following monikers for Jesus in the Book of Revelation sparks deeper reflection for you:
Alpha and Omega, root and offspring of David, or bright morning star?
Explain.

Prayer

Righteous Father, the world does not know you, but Jesus did know you and made you known to his disciples. Grant that your saints may lead us into deeper faith that we may know the Alpha and Omega, the root and offspring of David, the bright morning star, your Son, who is blessed with you, Holy Father, and the Holy Spirit, one God, forever and ever. Amen.

List of Hymns

Alleluia! Sing to Jesus
All Glory, Praise, and Honor
All Hail the Power of Jesus' Name
Angels from the Realms of Glory
At the Lamb's High Feast We Sing
At the Name of Jesus
Be Joyful, Mary, Heav'ly Queen
Blessed Feasts of Blessed Martyrs
Come, Holy Ghost, Creator Blest
Come, Our Almighty King
Crown Him with Many Crowns
Faith of Our Fathers
For All the Saints
Forty Days and Forty Nights
Hail the Day That Sees Him Rise
Hear Us, Almighty Lord
Holy God, We Praise Thy Name
Holy, Holy, Holy!
Jesus Christ Is Risen Today
Let All Mortal Flesh Keep Silence
Lord, Who throughout These Forty Days
On Jordan's Bank the Baptist's Cry
O Sacred Head, Surrounded
O Sons and Daughters
Praise to the Holiest in the Height
Shepherd of Souls
Songs of Thankfulness and Praise

List of Hymns

Take Up Your Cross
The Church's One Foundation
The King of Love My Shepherd Is
There's A Wideness in God's Mercy
The Strife Is O'er, the Battle Done
What Wondrous Love Is This?
When I Survey the Wondrous Cross
Were You There When They Crucified My Lord?

Other Books by Mark G. Boyer

History of St. Joachim Parish: 1822—1972; 1723—1973
Day by Day through the Easter Season
Following the Star: Daily Reflections for Advent and Christmas
Mystagogy: Liturgical Paschal Spirituality for Lent and Easter
Return to the Lord: A Lenten Journey of Daily Reflections
The Liturgical Environment: What the Documents Say
Breathing Deeply of God's New Life: Preparing Spiritually for the Sacraments of Initiation
Mary's Day—Saturday: Meditations for Marian Celebrations
Why Suffer?: The Answer of Jesus
A Month-by-Month Guide to Entertaining Angels
Biblical Reflections on Male Spirituality
"Seeking Grace with Every Step": The Spirituality of John Denver
Home Is a Holy Place
Day by Ordinary Day with Mark
Day by Ordinary Day with Matthew
Day by Ordinary Day with Luke
Baptized into Christ's Death and Resurrection: Preparing to Celebrate a Christian Funeral: Vol. 1: Adults
Baptized into Christ's Death and Resurrection: Preparing to Celebrate a Christian Funeral: Vol. 2: Children
The Greatest Gift of All: Reflections and Prayers for the Christmas Season
Meditations for Ministers
Waiting in Joyful Hope: Reflections for Advent 2001
Filled with New Light: Reflections for Christmas 2001–2002
Lent and Easter Prayer at Home
Using Film to Teach New Testament

Other Books by Mark G. Boyer

Waiting in Joyful Hope: Daily Reflections for Advent and Christmas 2002–2003
Waiting in Joyful Hope: Daily Reflections for Advent and Christmas 2003–2004
The Liturgical Environment: What the Documents Say (second edition)
Reflections on the Rosary
When Day Is Done: Nighttime Prayers through the Church Year
Take Up Your Cross and Follow: Daily Lenten Reflections
These Thy Gifts: A Collection of Simple Meal Prayers
Day by Ordinary Day: Daily Reflections on the First Readings, Year One
Day by Ordinary Day: Daily Reflections on the First Readings, Year Two
Mountain Reflections: A Collection of Photos and Meditations
Nature Spirituality: Praying with Wind, Water, Earth, Fire
A Spirituality of Ageing
Caroling through Advent and Christmas
Weekday Saints: Reflections on Their Scriptures
Human Wholeness: A Spirituality of Relationship
The Liturgical Environment: What the Documents Say (third edition)
A Simple Systematic Mariology
Praying Your Way through Luke's Gospel and the Acts of the Apostles
An Abecedarian of Animal Spirit Guides: Spiritual Growth through Reflections on Creatures

www.ingramcontent.com/pod-product-compliance
Lightning Source LLC
Chambersburg PA
CBHW062018220426
43662CB00010B/1378